CSLAs for Cybersecurity Professionals

A Guide to Cloud Service Agreements for the 21st Century

Includes Suggested Service Level Objectives (SLO) and Checklist

Mark A. Russo

CISSP-ISSAP, ITIL v3

Copyright 2018, Syber Risk LLC
Washington, DC ⊕ Tucson

DEDICATION

This book is dedicated to the cyber-security men and women that protect and defend the Information Systems of this great Nation.

Also, to my great friends and colleagues at the F-35 Joint Strike Fighter Program that must fight daily with the ignorance and obstinance toward the true meaning of "cybersecurity": keeping our men and women in uniform alive on the battlefield, in the sea, in the air...and in cyberspace

Copyright 2018, by Syber Risk LLC

LEGAL STUFF

Any registered ® named system, hardware or software component identified is only meant for educational purposes and does not construe any promotion of the product. Readers should exercise their due diligence and conduct proper market research to identify their needed products in accordance with their company or agency policies and standards.

This publication is not intended to provide any legal advice. It based upon current cybersecurity best-practices of the National Institute of Standards and Technology (NIST) and Department of Defense (DOD) standards as defined within the current implementation of the Risk Management Framework (RMF).

The author and publisher are providing best-practice and reasonable conclusions for the implementation of all solutions described. The author and publisher do not offer any warranty to the reader of the final outcomes based upon the ever-changing guidance promulgated by the US government. This is a good-faith effort to provide the best and most current information to companies and businesses in a highly dynamic area of US national and international concern, cybersecurity.

Special credit to the European Commission, Cloud Select Industry Group – Subgroup on Service Level Agreement (C-SIG-SLA). The C-SIG SLA subgroup, an industry group facilitated by the European Commission DG Connect, prepared a set of SLA standardization guidelines for cloud service providers and professional cloud service customers, while ensuring the specific needs of the European cloud market and industry. This book leverages and further refines many of those suggestions and findings to create a more definitive guide for businesses, cybersecurity professionals, and policy makers alike.

CSLAs for Cybersecurity Professionals

Table of Contents

SECTION 1: WELCOME TO THE CLOUD

The CIA Jumps into the Cloud

This chapter is designed to provide a short discussion of the hard and soft skills' challenges facing anyone intending to implement a cloud solution. We discuss the recent move by the Central Intelligence Agency (CIA) to rapidly initiate a cloud solution for the entirety of the multi-billion-dollar intelligence operations of the US. This chapter is meant to provide a short and current history of a massive cloud endeavor on the part of the CIA and some of the potential pitfalls facing others seeking cloud as a viable IT solution.

The ability to expand and contract computer resources and services provides direct benefit to a cash-strapped US federal government over the past several decades. The US's Intelligence Community (IC), for example, overall "[Information Technology] IT spending reached $8 billion in 2013" (Konkel, 2014, p.32). Cloud provides a means to consolidate costs, and more effectively execute cost-sharing across the IT enterprise. Cost savings is a major objective of pursuing cloud computing, and further derives an additional beneficial cost-sharing environment.

Cloud computing is a direct driver to needed cost efficiencies where, for example, licensing and budget limitations may exist for software tools. Cloud services that include software support would afford agencies the ability to share capabilities across bureaucratic governmental department lines. If the Department of Homeland Security (DHS) only needed 9 of 10 available software tool licenses, the State Department would not have to go through the typical elongated federal procurement process; it would just negotiate licenses with DHS to have access to the remaining license.

In *"Building the Infrastructure for Cloud Security: A Solution View"*, it stated that "[c]loud technology enables the disaggregation of computer, network, and storage resources in a data center into pools of resources, as well as the partitioning and re-aggregation of these resources according to the needs of the consumers down the supply chain" (Yeluria and Castro-Leon, 2014, p. 6). The important fact is that the distribution and redistribution of critical computer resources and software are significant to the user. The focus of any technologic solution must be its support and augmentation to people and mission; this aspect of cloud services is probably its greatest benefit.

On the negative side of the cloud "debate" while cost is a major concern, the CIA is reportedly executing a $600 million contract with Amazon to develop a private cloud solution; however, it will in fact result in greater <u>initial</u> start-up costs and most likely will impact the overall deployment timeline. A cloud solution, especially a private cloud, will be more expensive. For example, the IC will have to maintain its legacy architectures simultaneously until its cloud architectures are operational and fully accredited. (*A note of concern to the reader looking at initial challenges as you transition to a cloud solution.*) "Convenience comes at a price, as users must now trust the provider to "get it right" and are largely helpless in the face of the providers failures" (Nanavati, Colp, Aiello and Warfield, 2014, p.71). The costs in both dollars and government resources will be extensive especially during a prolonged developmental phase requiring multiple infrastructures and support contracts to remain in place.

Another significant weakness facing cloud computing implementation is its overall vulnerability to attack. In the article, "Committed to Cloud Computing," it expressed the serious concerns of cloud employment combining vast amounts of national security data and intelligence which: "... also means greater vulnerabilities" (Seffers, 2013, p.23). Cloud computing concentrates data in fewer locations allowing an attacker the ability to better focus his finite energy against fewer targets. The attacker can now consolidate his precious resources against fewer cloud locations vice a large array of data centers across the US.

In terms of 'process,' cloud solutions must be refined as situations and circumstances change especially with regards to new technologies. Cloud computing is a medium for processing, storage, and communications. It will not resolve issues of the people nor process components, and it will not directly or unilaterally affect change without human input. "Clouds do not automatically solve any information sharing policy or [other] change" (INSA White Paper, 2012, p.13). Only the creative or innovative people component can solve such issues. Process or policy refinement is a responsibility of the leadership and people who will implement cloud.

An interview of Carson Sweet, CEO of Cloud Passage, a cloud security provider, highlighted a cross-component need of secure cloud development as it relates to the IC's implementation of cloud computing. In the article, "Cloud Security," he identified an area where both IC leadership and well-developed contractual requirements must be established between the IC and Amazon. He recognized that: "there's a shared responsibility Amazon's EC2 [cloud solution] ... will take care of part of the security. The owner of the virtual machines will have to do the rest" (Holbrook, 2012, p. 12). Leadership will need to ensure that its development and oversight of this contract is thorough in considering the governments past inability to execute IT contracts to include, for example, the poor recent deployment of Healthcare.gov in conjunction with the "Affordable Care Act" (ACA).

With the currently available public information regarding this effort, it is uncertain that the IC is well-prepared to execute cloud computing successfully. Even the National Security Agency's (NSA) Chief Information Officer(CIO) stated that: "...officials have no set date by which they will reach full operational capability" (Seffers, 2013, p.23). This adds to the concern that the IC, specifically, has not adequately planned its cloud development and implementation efforts.

Furthermore, in this brief example from within the US government, technology alone cannot be used to solve shortfalls. Another serious weakness has been the lack of thoughtful analysis of cloud computing benefits and especially risks. The most disconcerting information from public references highlights an almost non-critical evaluation of the employment of cloud. Former CIA cybersecurity researcher, John Pirc, expressed that since the CIA was totally accepting cloud computing that this was rationale enough to prove that cloud computing was secure. "To me, this [the CIA executing a cloud contract] … removes the clouded judgment that cloud isn't secure" (Konkel, 2014, p. 34). This statement <u>cannot</u> be used to validate that cloud is secure just because the CIA has accepted it. (*The logic here totally escapes the author on this quote*). Both the Konkel (2014) and Seffers (2013) references highlight an almost inept understanding and planning effort to conduct a cloud computing transition. Furthermore, there are no substantive assurances from these direct interviews with IC leadership that confidentiality, integrity, or availability have been fully considered.

There is no "magic bullet" that a cloud architecture provides absolute and concrete security to the overall IT environment. It is just another form of distributed IT network infrastructure requiring the same concerns and oversight to ensure that both the functionality and security are met through a cloud implementation. The Cloud Service Level Agreement (CSLA) plays a serious role in identifying the demarcation of responsibilities between the System Owner and the Cloud Service Provider (CSP); if not tightly managed it may lead to loss of sensitive data, Intellectual Property (IP), and reputation on the part of the System Owner alone. While the CSP may be *responsible* for its portion of security controls, it is the System Owner that is overall *accountable* to the board of directors, stakeholders, and taxpayers for the strengths and weaknesses of a cloud solution.

Cybersecurity Systems Hardening

Cloud is no different than any other computer-based IT infrastructure or environment. It is composed of multiple hardware devices, servers, routers, etc. This includes software of various types to include Operating Systems, applications, firmware, etc., that all potentially expose varied vulnerabilities until discovered and made public. The CIA is only one of many examples of the hype outpacing the reality and true capabilities of cloud.

One of those immediate security challenges facing cloud implementation is misconfiguration of cloud platforms. This is not unique to the cloud phenomenon. There are numerous major private companies and defense contractors stating they are "cybersecurity experts," and that is unfortunately an abject lie. A vast majority will deploy servers and software "out of the box" with no consideration to hardening protocols either as found within DOD's Security Technical Implementation Guides (STIG) or NIST maintained "National Checklist Program Repository" site at https://nvd.nist.gov/ncp/repository . This includes, for example, not changing factory set passwords. The hacking community has a large library that provides insight to these publicly known and easily exploited vulnerabilities. The failure is widespread, and cloud is just the most public.

In 2018, misconfiguration of cloud platforms was the biggest global threat to cloud deployment. A recent survey by Crowd Research Partners, **"Cloud Security Report,"** (https://www.cybersecurity-insiders.com/portfolio/2018-cloud-security-report-download/) states 62% of its respondents believed it was the number one threat. This is also followed by improper access controls at 55% which is also a function of improper configurations creating additional susceptibility and concern by the cybersecurity community.

Security continues to be a major concern and will not change until CSP's understand their roles and responsibilities in creating a secure environment. It is not a once and done approach. CSPs must integrate the hardening of its hardware and software as part of its active lifecycle and continuous monitoring processes.

It begins with identifying the hardware and software inventory of the CSP. This should include all Operating systems, applications, makes and models of hardware such as firewalls, servers, routers, etc.; this information will provide the CSP with the requisite start point to select the proper STIGs or NIST-based security settings that they provide for a wider and more public audience. These listings are the foundation of not just "systems hardening management" processes but is an integral part of configuration management and continuous monitoring activities that are the base principles of NIST's Risk Management Framework (RMF) -- What you don't know can truly hurt you.

We have outlined a five-step approach to creating an effective systems hardening process. It includes:

1. **STEP 1: Identifying Inventory.** This should be a complete hardware and software listing of all devices and software in the cloud environment. This should include a detailed listing because when the CSP reaches Step 2 of the process, the CSP

can easily determine whether there is an applicable STIG or NIST checklist that is already available.

2. **STEP 2: Identifying Hardening Guides.** This will either be from STIGS (if supporting a DOD-based cloud hosting effort), or NIST policy and configuration setting guides found in its "National Checklist Program Repository." If they exist in either environment, they will be the basis of secure configuration settings for hardware and software. If one does not exist, then the CSP should notify the Cloud Service Customer (CSC) and propose alternate means. This may take the form of creating a CSP-created "STIG" or, at a minimum, apply a best practice regime to ensure security is adequately met. (A suggested "Alternate Cybersecurity Systems Hardening Best Practices Checklist can be found at Appendix B.)

3. **STEP 3: Apply Security Settings.** Apply settings as recommended using the manual checklists. There are some hardening approaches that use automated setup; this will require additional tools and expertise, but in most instances, this will increase the speed of configuration changes and increase security. Subsequently, ensure all changes are documented. This should include filled out checklists (manual) or printouts (automated) of the completed setting changes.

4. **STEP 4: Quality Assurance (QA).** One of the often-missed part of any process within cybersecurity is QA. This should include not only CSP review, CSC oversight of the changes, but, where possible, should include third-party QA entities. This could include members of the CSC's cybersecurity staff that verifies that the security policy and configuration changes have been implemented. There should be recurring spot-checks on either a regular basis (e.g., quarterly) or ad hoc as defined in the CSLA.

5. **STEP 5: Log Changes.** At this final phase, the system hardening effort should parallel like "recurring" and "standing" security workflows such as "Patch Management" or "White/Blacklisting Updates and Changes." These changes typically require less scrutiny for implementation, but there should be minimal review by authorized CSP personnel to authorize the change.

We have prepared a **"Standard Cybersecurity Systems Hardening Workflow"** (Chart 1) below to assist the CSP and CSC have a better understanding of the process and how best to employ it in an active cloud environment. While this chapter was created to better assist the CSP, it is also helpful to the CSC in understanding the secure policy and configuration settings that will best protect sensitive data within a cloud solution. It is partitioned based upon whether the CSP is supporting a DOD cloud deployment or non-DOD agency and can include private businesses seeking to ensure security protections by the CSP are complete.

After the inventory has been completed, if supporting the DOD, the CSP will be able to leverage DOD's STIG database for hardware and software policy and configurations settings. More typically, NIST's "National Checklist Repository" will be the more likely location for such settings. Typically, the CSP will have to first assemble its on-staff experts to organize and execute the configuration settings on all hardware devices. All servers, routers, firewalls, etc., should be set as soon as possible. All default settings, especially passwords, should be reset, documented, and securely stored for reference by CSP IT support personnel. **The National Repository** may redirect users to other sites to include, for example, DOD's own STIG database or the CIS Benchmarks' site (https://www.cisecurity.org/cis-benchmarks/).

Software, to include Operating Systems (OS), applications, databases, etc., will require hardening once the network architecture is assembled by the CSP. CSP's will typically use manual checklists, but in some cases will use automated tools that that will establish secure policy and configuration settings. These actions may require additional expertise.

Step 3 should be an ongoing activity and be an integral part of the CSP's Continuous Monitoring (ConMon) plan.[1] Hardening settings are constantly being updated. Much like Original Equipment Manufacturer (OEM) patch updates, they may be periodic or aperiodic, and issued at different times. The CSP will have to establish a review process where their IT staff are reviewing the varied databases on a weekly basis, at minimum. Hardening setting changes can change typically every several months either when around a new version (software) or hardware upgrade (firmware) that will require a process that demonstrates "due diligence" to the CSC, auditors, and the government, as required.

Continuous Monitoring's (ConMon) Role

 *The Committee on National Security Systems defines ConMon as: "[t]he processes implemented to maintain current security status for one or more information systems on which the operational mission of the enterprise depends," (CNSS, 2010). ConMon has been described as the holistic solution of end-to-end cybersecurity coverage and the answer to providing an effective global Risk Management (RM)*

solution.

For ConMon to become a reality for any business or agency, it must meet the measures and expectations as defined in National Institute of Standards and Technology (NIST) Special Publication (SP) 800-137. "Continuous monitoring has evolved as a best practice for managing

---

[1] Systems hardening settings are a key part of a well-established "continuous monitoring" program as defined in NIST 800-137, "Information Security Continuous Monitoring for Federal Information Systems and Organizations."

risk on an ongoing basis," (SANS Institute, 2016); it is an instrument that supports effective, continual, and recurring RM assurances. For any agency to truly espouse it has attained full compliance, it must be able to coordinate all the listed major elements as found in NIST SP 800-137.

It is not just the passive visibility pieces, but also includes the active efforts of vulnerability scanning, threat alert, reduction, mitigation, or elimination of a dynamic IT environment. This framework addresses how an agency would approach identifying a ConMon solution. Finally, it requires alignment with the "11 Security Automation Domains" that are necessary to implement true ConMon.

The 11 Security Automation Domains (NIST, 2011)

Always critical within the area of cybersecurity is well-kept records and documentation. This can include the actual checklists, print-outs, etc., with some form of attestation by the individual or individuals responsible for executing policy settings. These will typically include System Administrators (SA) and Database Administrators (DBA) with elevated privileges to implement the settings. These individuals should also have basic knowledge of especially the OS and major applications to implement these changes effectively and completely.

In Step 4, there should be a Quality Assurance (QA) review. While RMF does allow for "self-assessment," we strongly disagree with this approach except under extreme circumstances. QA can be afforded by third-party auditors either from the CSC's own IT staff or contracted auditors who can provide an assessment of the completeness and accuracy of the policy and security settings. QA should be done before allowing "live" data becoming operational. Where that is not possible, a Plan of Action and Milestones (POAM) should be documented to ensure the issue is tracked and corrected soon; **this is the very core of what NIST Risk Management is all about.**

Once this step is completed it should be reviewed by the individual or organization charged with monitoring Configuration Management (CM). Assuming the policy settings have not created a negative operational impact, i.e., it has not broken operational functionality, it should be signed and attested by the CM agent and entered in the CM database; the CM database is the final repository for changes and should be used as an archival storage of all changes for the CSP and its respective cloud environments.

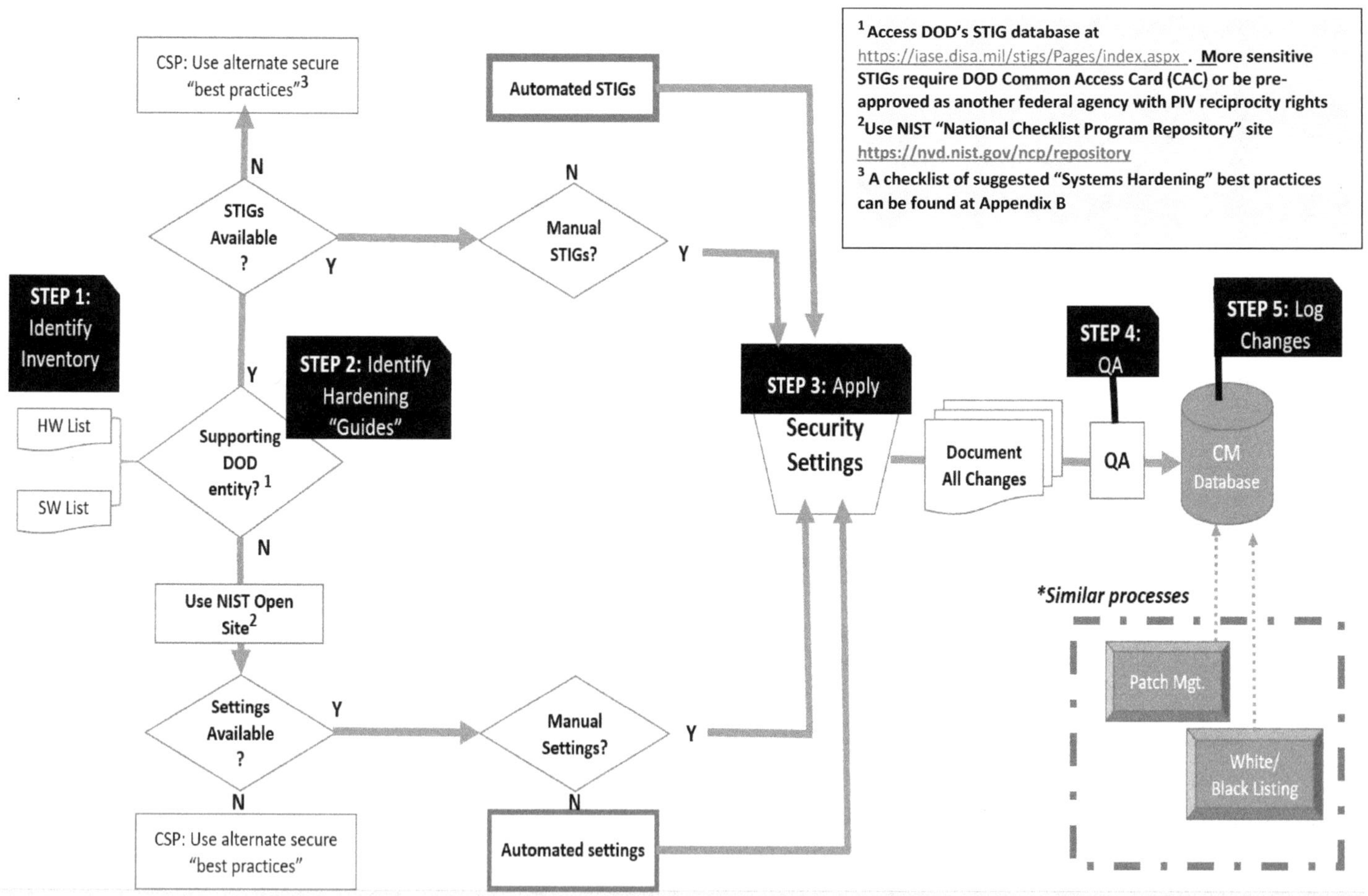
CSP: Use alternate secure "best practices"[3]
Automated STIGs
N
STIGs Available ?
Y
Manual STIGs?
Y
STEP 1: Identify Inventory
HW List
SW List
Supporting DOD entity? [1]
STEP 2: Identify Hardening "Guides"
N
Use NIST Open Site[2]
Settings Available ?
Y
Manual Settings?
Y
N
N
CSP: Use alternate secure "best practices"
Automated settings
STEP 3: Apply
Security Settings
Document All Changes
STEP 4: QA
QA
STEP 5: Log Changes
CM Database
*Similar processes
Patch Mgt.
White/ Black Listing
[1] Access DOD's STIG database at https://iase.disa.mil/stigs/Pages/index.aspx . More sensitive STIGs require DOD Common Access Card (CAC) or be pre-approved as another federal agency with PIV reciprocity rights
[2] Use NIST "National Checklist Program Repository" site https://nvd.nist.gov/ncp/repository
[3] A checklist of suggested "Systems Hardening" best practices can be found at Appendix B

Chart 1: Standard Cybersecurity Systems Hardening

The Cloud & Cloud Security

This book is written to address a vital component of Cloud Security, the **Service Level Agreement (SLA).** While many of us who work in the cybersecurity realm agree that the SLA is a critical artifact in determining third-party responsibility for the implementation of security controls, there is very little information on what a good SLA consists of. This book is written for that very purpose. If you are writing or reviewing a **Cloud SLA (CSLA)**, or a standard Information Technology (IT) SLA, what are the elements needed to effectively have a good service agreement? What are the kinds of **Service Level Objectives** (SLO) do you need to manage as a company or agency to ensure your overall shared cybersecurity responsibilities are being met? This book is written to provide a how-to approach to better understand the place and importance of the CSLA. This is written for the Cybersecurity Professional or consultant looking for the right resource to help guide their efforts. This book focuses on the specific solution or resource locations to ensure that the customers' needs are being met when moving to a cloud environment.

We have attempted to gather the most current information both from the United States (US) and internationally that has sought to address the critical components of an effective CSLA. We discuss its general role within companies and organizations, and how to recognize what "good" looks like. The goal of this book is to provide a comprehensive resource to enumerate, select, and administer an effective third-party quality assurance checklist to improve the state of the current and far-reaching implementation of cloud solutions for both the public and private sectors. This book will provide a baseline understanding of how to get the job done and done well.

Another purpose of this book is to address the expected US federal government expansion of the National Institute of Standards and Technology (NIST) Special Publication (SP) 800-171, revision 1, ***Protecting Unclassified Information in Nonfederal Information Systems and Organizations.*** It ultimately will require that any company, business, or agency, supporting the US Government is fully compliant with NIST 800-171 no later than the date of contract award, and that includes any full or partial use of a cloud solution—we have a devoted a chapter to that discussion.

While there is yet to be a final determination of a wide-ranging requirement for those contractors providing goods and services to the federal government being impacted, the Federal Acquisition Regulation (FAR) Committee's Case # 2017-016 had an original suspense date to make a formal recommendation to the President by March 2018; that date has come and gone. The latest and expected timeframe for any final decision has moved to an expected timeframe of November/December 2018. While it is possible that the Federal Acquisition Regulation (FAR) Committee may further delay its NIST 800-171 expansion recommendation, and the Administration may subsequently delay its implementation to 2019, the value and the purpose of this book is no less critical in its discussion of the CSLA.

Cloud computing is composed of four essential characteristics. They include:

1. **Resource pools** which are available collections of capabilities and functionalities required to maintain a company or agency's services as well as more specifically its cybersecurity posture.

2. **On-demand self-services** that provide the granular elasticity to expand and contract operations in near-real time that is controllable by the customer or System Owner (SO).

3. **Broad network access** which leverages a CSP's larger organic and expansive infrastructure without requiring additional time and resources on the part of the Cloud Service Customer (CSC).

4. **Measured Services** that collect data and metrics to determine the Quality of Service (QOS) provided by and to the customer.

Implementation Offerings & Deployment Models

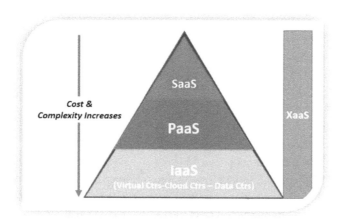

Cloud Implementation Standard Services Model

There are four service models for cloud implementation.

1. **Software as a Service (SaaS):** The capability provided to the cloud service customer is to use the CSP's applications (e.g., word processing, spreadsheet, financial, and human resource) running on a cloud infrastructure. The applications are typically accessible from various client devices through a thin-client interface, such as a web browser (e.g. web-based email). (See Appendix A for a more complete explanation of terminology.)

2. **Platform as a Service (PaaS):** The capability provided to the cloud customer to deploy onto a cloud infrastructure "customer-created" or acquired applications created using modern programming languages, libraries, services, and tools supported by the CSP; these are usually company-tailored applications specific to a unique requirement for that organization and need the proper IT environment that the company or organization cannot develop or maintain organically.

3. **Infrastructure as a Service (IaaS):** The capability provided to the cloud customer to provide processing, storage, networks, and other fundamental computing resources where the cloud service customer can deploy and run arbitrary software, which can include operating systems and applications. This is a much broader model to house an external and complete IT infrastructure that cannot be maintained or funded by the agency directly. Mostly used to reduce overall IT operations' costs.

4. **Anything as a Service (XaaS):** A collective term of diverse but *re-useable* components, including infrastructure, platforms, data, software, middleware, hardware or other goods, made available as a service. This affords a more "ala carte" approach where services and capabilities can be selected as needed and terminated or reduced based upon operational necessity or cost.

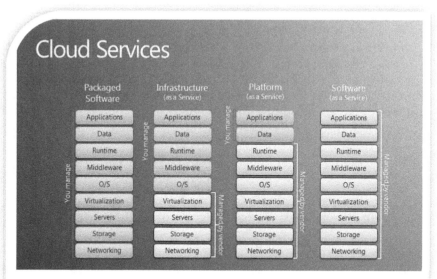

Table 2, Notional Division of Security Inheritance and Risk (Source: DoD Cloud Computing SRG)

There are four cloud deployment models. They are the:

1. Community Cloud
2. Public Cloud
3. Hybrid Cloud
4. Private Cloud

They all have their own advantages and disadvantages in terms of complexity, cost, and flexibility. Considerations of the deployment model should be based primarily on the sensitivity of the *data* (e.g., Controlled Unclassified Information (CUI), Critical Defense Information (CDI), etc.) and the threats against the company or agency based upon current threat information, intelligence and understanding of the overall IT environment.

CSLA Considerations

The CSLA further defines the terms and conditions for access and use of the services offered by the CSP. It specifically establishes the service terms, conditions for termination, and disposition of data (e.g., media protection preservation, maintenance, and destruction policies and procedures) during the period of the contract or upon contract and CSLA termination. The complete terms and conditions for a cloud service agreement are typically captured in multiple documents, but the most significant document is the CSLA. The CSLA, *as part of a well-executed contract*, is the basis of a good cloud security employment. The subsequent guidance and suggested Service Level Objectives (SLO) in Sections 2 and 3 are designed to be the basis of an effective overall cloud implementation.

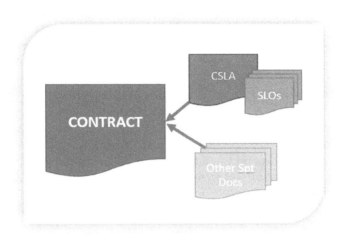

Base Cloud Service Suggested Documents

The CSLA characterizes the understanding between the customer[2] (business or agency) and CSP about the expected level of service to be delivered. If the CSP fails to deliver the service at the level specified, there is a credit or refund that occurs based upon the level and duration of shortfall resulting from the CSP's inability to fully deliver on the stated level or Quality of Service (QOS) provisions. (See Appendix B for a Sample Cloud Service Level Agreement).

Additionally, there are two types of service agreements: 1) "non-negotiable" agreements and "negotiated" agreements. Non-negotiable agreements are in many ways the basis for much of the discussion of the major advantages of cloud, and its economies of scale sought by public cloud computing advocates. The terms of service are prescribed *completely* by the cloud provider. They are typically not written with attention to specific federal privacy and security requirements. Furthermore, with some offerings, the provider can make modifications

---

[2] The term "customer", "cloud customer," and "System Owner (SO)" should be considered equivalent for the purposes of this book; they are all ultimately accountable for the security posture of their respective company or agency.

to the terms of service unilaterally (e.g., by posting an updated version online at their respective website) without providing any direct notification to the cloud consumer.

"Negotiated" service agreements are more traditional outsourcing contracts for IT services. **This should be the objective course for any organization seeking partial or full transition to a cloud service environment.** They can be used to address an organization's specific and "ala carte" concerns about, for example, security and privacy policies, procedures, and technical controls. This could include the vetting of employees, data ownership, breach notifications, isolation of tenant applications, data encryption and overall compliance with international, US federal, state, and local laws specific to cybersecurity protections and execution. It may also require the use of applied cybersecurity standards such as Security Technical Implementation Guidance (STIG) or validated product certifications meeting national or international standards, e.g., Federal Information Processing Standard (FIPS) 140-2 for cryptographic modules.

More critical data and applications require an agency to undertake a negotiated service agreement. Since points of negotiation can impact cost and negatively affect the economies of scale that a non-negotiable service agreement brings to public cloud computing, a negotiated service agreement is typically less cost effective. Furthermore, while it may be less cost effective, it can be used to prioritize control protections by the CSP based upon budgeting constraints. It may in fact be a better choice based upon the sensitivity of the data and the company or agencies requirements to ensure overall cybersecurity readiness.

The outcome of a negotiation is dependent on the size of the organization and its ability to exert influence upon the CSP. Regardless of the type of agreement obtaining adequate legal and technical advice is recommended to ensure that the terms of service meet the needs of the organization and the required levels of data security protection required under the law.

Accountability versus Responsibility

The Executive Order #13800, "Strengthening the Cybersecurity of Federal Networks and Critical Infrastructure" signed in May 2018 held all federal executive branch secretaries *accountable* for agency information security management, governance, and policy; the "buck" was truly placed upon all secretaries and holds them to task to ensure the cybersecurity readiness of their respective agencies.

There are two major participants in a CSLA. They are the Cloud Service Customer (CSC), also called the System Owner (SO), and the Cloud Service Provider (CSP). Typically, the "accountability" for the effective implementation of security controls solely resides with the SO. (See examples of common security controls below.) While the SO is accountable, the CSP is "responsible" for those controls identified specifically within the CSLA; that is why the CSLA is so important to be as complete and thorough as possible. While the CSP will be held to meeting the terms of the CSLA, the SO is always accountable for the completeness and certainty that every control is implemented properly; it is never an excuse to place blame on the CSP when an intrusion or violation occurs. The SO with its organic contract and IT support staffs must understand, draft, and properly oversee its CSLA's terms and conditions with respect to the CSP continuously.

NIST SP 800-53 revision 4

EXAMPLE SECURITY CONTROLS DERIVED FROM NIST 800-53 revision 4, "Security and Privacy Controls for Federal Information Systems and Organizations", February 2012:

AC-1 ACCESS CONTROL POLICY AND PROCEDURES

Control: The organization develops, disseminates, and reviews/updates [Assignment: organization defined frequency]:

a. A formal, documented access control policy that addresses purpose, scope, roles, responsibilities, management commitment, coordination among organizational entities, and compliance; and

b. Formal, documented procedures to facilitate the implementation of the access control policy and associated access controls.

CM-9 CONFIGURATION MANAGEMENT PLAN

The organization develops, documents, and implements a configuration management plan for the information system that:

a. Addresses roles, responsibilities, and configuration management processes and procedures;

b. Establishes a process for identifying configuration items throughout the system development life cycle and for managing the configuration of the configuration items;

c. Defines the configuration items for the information system and places the configuration items under configuration management.

IR-5 INCIDENT MONITORING:

The organization tracks and documents information system security incidents.

Supplemental Guidance: Documenting information system security incidents includes, for example, maintaining records about each incident, the status of the incident, and other pertinent information necessary for forensics, evaluating incident details, trends, and handling. Incident information can be obtained from a variety of sources including, for example, incident reports, incident response teams, audit monitoring, network monitoring, physical access monitoring, and user/administrator reports.

Finally, any cloud implementation is no more secure than any standard architecture. It must be managed as any IT infrastructure constantly shifting with changing threats and risks. The sole accountability remains with the SO, i.e., the customer. If there is a failure in protecting its most sensitive data, the fault will lie with this senior corporate official designated. This book is written to provide a needed resource to ensure the protection of vital and sensitive public and private data. Any failure of cybersecurity is not the fault of cybersecurity specialists and IT support staffs, it is a failure of the leadership; accountability must rest with the leadership always.

The CSLA

The CSLA forms an important component of the contractual relationship between a cloud customer and a CSP. Given the global nature of the cloud, CSLAs usually span many jurisdictions with often varying applicable legal requirements with respect to the protection of the sensitive and personal data hosted in the cloud. Differing cloud services and deployment models require varied approaches to CSLAs which adds to the complexity. CSLA terminology often differs from one CSP to another making it difficult for cloud customers to compare varied cloud service offerings. Standardizing the CSLA improves its clarity and increases the understanding of the cloud service market.

There is a clear need for cloud guidelines and standardization of CSLA for contracts between CSP and CSC. In February 2013, the European Commission established the Cloud Select Industry Group – Subgroup on Service Level Agreement (C-SIG-SLA). Their objective was to establish standardization. They attempted to begin defining the groundwork for CSLA standardization at the international level rather than specific to any national or regional "stove piped" initiative. This book leverages that work and enhances its usability and guidance for the business leader and their IT support staff seeking to grasp the challenges posed by an effective CSLA. The objective is to provide for a holistic implementation to avoid any surprises to the cloud service-seeking community. The following standards and principles are meant to provide a deeper understanding of that challenge.

1. Technology Agnostic or Neutral

Essential parts of cloud computing are its flexibility and extensibility for which technology neutrality is a necessary foundation. Cloud services can be built using any number of available and modern technologies. For example, many cloud services publicly "expose" **Representational State Transfer** (REST)[3] interfaces or *Application Programming Interfaces* (API)[4] , but they can also use technologies such as Web Services to receive data to interoperate with other services. Technology neutrality is important because cloud services commonly run on virtualized hardware platforms, but virtualization should *not* be assumed.

Continuous improvement to deliver increasing value is critical to the future of cloud computing and the freedom to innovate technically is key. Cloud services are built on open source software and proprietary software alike. There can also be a variety of hardware platforms underlying cloud services.

---

[3] "A software architectural style consisting of a coordinated set of architectural constraints applied to components, connectors, and data elements, within a distributed system."
[4] "A collection of methods and associated parameters used by a cloud service or software component to request actions from and otherwise interact with another cloud service or software component."

2. Business Model Neutral

A business model for cloud services should not be assumed. Cloud services may be funded by any number of methods such as pay per use, long term contracts, advertising, public funds, etc. Remedies for failure to achieve cloud SLO stated in the CSLA can also take different forms such as refunds, free services or other forms of compensation.

3. General Applicability

The Internet is a global communications channel and it is built on standards that are respected worldwide. Likewise, cloud services have a global audience of governments, small businesses, enterprises, Non-Governmental Organizations (NGOs) and individuals. Agreements that govern cloud services must account for regional, national and local laws, regulations and policies; everyone should benefit from globally common concepts, vocabularies and accessible technologies.

4. Explicit Definitions

Keeping the definition of SLOs well-defined and unambiguous is important to ensure the effective standardization of CSLAs and enable clear communication between CSP and CSC. As technology progresses and new terminology is developed, it will also be important to ensure definitions are current and consistent with an evolving cloud services landscape.

5. Service Level Objectives

SLO are often quantitative and have related measurements. For CSC to make informed decisions when choosing cloud services, it is best if the offered SLO can be easily compared. Measurements should also be comparable since reduced comparability hampers acceptance. When reviewing and analyzing less-quantitative or qualitative SLOs and comparing different services may provide extra insights for making such informed decisions.

SLOs need not be determined by identical means but sufficient information about the SLO needs to be provided by CSPs. Standardized terminology, metrics and templates can be helpful in documenting how an SLO has been created and determined in meeting security and functionality demands of the customer.

SLOs are often associated with metrics. A metric is a defined measurement method and measurement scale which is used in relation to a quantitative SLO. Metrics are used to set the boundaries and margins of errors which apply to the behavior of the cloud service and any limitations. Metrics may be used at runtime for service monitoring, balancing, or remediation. Using a standard set of metrics or metric templates in the CSLA makes it easier and faster to define a CSLA and SLOs; it simplifies the task of comparing one CSLA to another.

6. Disclosure

Since standards and guidelines for CSLAs should be technology and business model neutral, they should not mandate a specific approach for any concept. For example, **service availability** can be measured differently. Some measurements will depend on the specific cloud service. A **computational service**[5] is different than a cloud email service which is different than service availability for each will be computed require greater of less complexities to computer processing, memory, and speed. CSPs should document their method of achieving SLOs for each concept in their CSLA based on a standard concept and vocabulary that is flexible enough to accommodate the various needs of their customer base.

7. Standards and Guidelines

Cloud services are valuable to both enterprises with millions of small businesses with fewer users and computing demands. The cloud service is a highly standardized offering that relies on uniformity to achieve desired economies of scale and offer customers benefits such as lower cost. In some cases, the CSLA and other governing documents, for example the System Security Plan (SSP) and Plan of Action and Milestones (POAM), etc., may be negotiated between the cloud service customer and the CSP. Negotiations cannot be assumed to always be favorable to the System Owner (SO)/customer. In many cases, CSC are may be offered a fixed standard agreement by the CSP which they may choose to accept or reject. The basis of any such decision should include wider access to CSP competition that best affords better terms of cost and completeness.

Standards and guidelines for CSLAs must be able to span from the smallest CSC to the largest. Useful standards and guidelines exist and are produced by several highly-regarded organizations such as the US's National Institute of Standards and Technology (NIST), The European Union Agency for Network and Information Security (ENISA), or International Organization for Standardization (ISO). For example, in the general field of cybersecurity there is an active movement to analyze, refine, and decompose specific security controls into one of more Security SLOs (SSLO). These SSLOs are then associated with metrics and measurements that can be either quantitative or qualitative.

---

[5] "Computational Services" provide higher processing and analytic capabilities not resident within the respective customer's internal IT infrastructure.

8. Proof Validation

Any effort to develop standards and guidelines for CSLAs should consider the state-of the-art and to some degree the representative capabilities of the cloud services industry. The state-of-the-art should not necessarily limit the introduction of new ideas or the re-use of long standing concepts, but they should be considered relative to industry's capabilities including the cloud essential characteristics. Before introducing a concept into a standard or guideline for CSLAs the organization should seek such "proof validation" measures to ensure the concept is viable from both technical and business perspectives.

9. Information versus Structure

Standards and guidelines for CSLAs should specify the structure of the CSLA. They should specify the security controls and concepts to maximize the security posture for the IT customer. Information helps business and technical stakeholders understand the nonlegal concepts and vocabulary used in CSLAs, and further provides a more complete solution for the business or agency.

Not all SLOs will be relevant for every cloud service. Some of the concepts mentioned in this document may not be part of the standard offering for all cloud computing services given the varied differences between cloud services models (i.e., IaaS, PaaS, SaaS, XaaS), as well as the many different cloud services provided within such groups of cloud services models. A non-implemented SLO does not imply that the service is of lower quality. There may be cases where similar information could be derived from other SLOs. It is important for the cloud service customer to understand the complete set of documents that govern the cloud service and to identify SLOs wherever they are required to protect their critical IT infrastructures, systems, or networks.

A CSLA can be a part of an overall **Master Service Agreement (MSA).** The CSLA specifically establishes the sought or required SLOs. However, the organization and the descriptions used for an MSA and its associated documents can vary considerably. It is may be further based upon the SLO service location within the document. These extra direct and indirect support documents should enhance the overall CSLA effort as appropriate; some of these documents demonstrate on behalf of the CSP their own internal compliance measures. These measures *should* be used by the CSC to assess the CSP's ability to support the business or agency seeking a viable cloud service. They may include:

- **Master Service Agreement (MSA)**
- **Service Level Agreement (SLA)**
- **Service Agreement**

- **Acceptable Use Policy** (control-related[6])

- **Privacy Policy** (control-related)

- **Security Policy** (control-related)

- **Business Continuity Policy** (control-related)

- **Service Description**

In this chapter, we covered the standards and principles that are vital to an effective CSLA implementation. Without establishing a standard lexicon and approach in the early phases of cloud services, the struggles of effectively employing cloud models will only be more difficult for both the general business and IT communities. This discussion was meant to provide a deeper understanding of the challenges facing both the CSC and CSP as they attempt to coordinate their actions to meet the objectives of functionality and security within their respective IT environments.

Types of CSLAs

There are two types of CSLA's that most likely will be the standard in the current cloud service provider marketplace. It will either be *ala carte* (select the controls singularly) or as part of a plan offering such as "bronze," "silver," or "platinum" offerings. No matter which type selected, remember the greater the number of controls selected, the greater the cost will be. While the expectation is that a company or agency using a cloud service will desire to have as many controls "exported" to a third-party CSP, the full cost may be prohibitive. It is important to consider the security budget first based upon what is reasonably affordable.

Also, identifying measurable Security Service Level Objectives (SSLO) in CSLAs are useful to improve both assurance and transparency to both the business or agency. However, just as important are the roles in the evolution of more expansive international, federal and state cybersecurity laws and regulations. Consideration must be made to ongoing changes to include a wider array of external stakeholders such as customers and outside inspectors destined to become a part of any security quality assurance oversight, evaluation and measures.[7]

CSLAs allow for establishing a common language for managing cloud security from two perspectives, specifically, 1) the security level being offered by a cloud service provider and, 2) the security level requested by a cloud service customer. The common terminology will help as

---

[6] "Control-related." These supplemental documents and their security applicability can be found specifically in NIST SP 800-53 revision 4.
[7] Expected future changes would occur requiring third-party assessors from either the government or contracted private companies. The likely emergence would occur because of a reported cybersecurity breach/attack raising a greater need for outside evaluations and forensic investigations.

the cloud becomes more common-place as such environments become more reliable, secure, and cost effective.

The approach used in this section consists of analyzing security controls from established security frameworks especially those formulated by NIST into additional SLOs, when appropriate. These SLOs can be either quantitative or qualitative. These sections focus on likely SLOs and suggested metrics that may meet the needs of the company or agency. Any determination of the kinds and numbers must be based on several factors:

1. **Cost:** Can the current budget support a complete or partial shift of security "responsibility" to a CSP?[8]

2. **The level of protections required for data:** How sensitive is the data? Does it include, for example, Personally Identifiable Information (PII) or Personal/Protected Health Information (PHI)?

3. **The threat landscapes:** What has been the general targeting of the specific industry by, for example, hackers, insider threats (e.g., disgruntled employees or corporate espionage) or nation-state actors?

4. **The risk to the company or agency's mission and reputation:** What is the impact to the company if it has repeatedly and unsuccessfully deterred or stopped unauthorized intrusions?

5. **The urgency to implement security:** Is there a current law, mandate or regulation requiring a rapid transition to a more secure IT environment, to include, cloud service?

The categories are representative of important functionality, service, and especially, security requirements. Not all security requirement categories are reflected. For example, resilience, business continuity and disaster recovery are important aspects of security not captured in this book. Specific controls and measures are usually put in place by CSPs, but no SLO has been derived for these additional security aspects; the CSC and IT Staff will have to determine proper additional SLOs based upon the security controls, for example, those selected during Step 1 of the NIST Risk Management Framework (RMF) process.

---

[8] *REMEMBER, as the System Owner YOU are ultimately accountable for data loss, not the CSP.*

CSLAs and DOD NIST 800-171

While NIST 800-series cybersecurity publications tell a business or agency "what" is required, they do not necessarily help in telling "how" to meet the security control requirements. The number of security controls may further increase based upon the actual or perceived threats. In the case of the likely expansion of NIST 800-171 to apply across the federal government in 2018-2019, it will be a major driver for companies to understand, formulate, and execute well-written CSLAs.

For example, NIST 800-171 applies to both **prime and their subcontractors**. There are three core contractual obligations that have been captured from both the FAR and the Defense Federal Acquisition Regulation Supplement (DFARS) specific to DOD contracting and in addition to the FAR:

1. "Adequately safeguard" Controlled Unclassified Information (CUI), and if working with the Department of Defense (DOD), Covered/Critical Defense Information (CDI).

2. Provide timely cyber-incident reporting to the government when an IT network breach is identified; typically, within 72 hours or sooner.

3. If operating with a CSP, "adequate" security needs to be demonstrated; usually through a contract with the CSP that shows that they are providing adequate security to provide data protection as a third-party service provider. CSLA should show the business is executing sound cybersecurity diligence to government Contract Officers (CO).

What is "adequate security?" **Adequate security** is defined by "compliance" specific in the case of the NIST 800-171 framework that has 110 defined and explicit security controls. This will also include when the CO has reviewed the security package and has issued the solicitation, i.e., contract award. This does not mean all security controls are in effect, but where a deviation is needed, a Plan of Action and Milestones (POAM) is provided.

A POAM is required as part of the official submission package to the government. It should identify why the company cannot currently address the control, and when it expects to resolve the control. (See the supplementary guide: *Writing an Effective Plan of Action & Milestones (POAM) available on Amazon® for further details.*)

The business is also required to provide timely cyber-incident reporting to the government when a breach into its network has occurred. The DOD requirement, for example, is that the business notifies the government within 72 hours upon ***recognition*** of a security incident.

Changing federal cybersecurity contract requirements are also taking into consideration the vast moves within the public and private sectors into cloud services. Typically, the security protections would be found in any contracts or CSLA between the business and the CSP. These are normally sufficient evidence for the government.

The good news regarding CSPs are there are many current CSPs that are already in compliance with the government's Federal Risk and Authorization Management Program (FedRAMP). Being FEDRAMP-compliant prior to final submission a NIST 800-171 Body of Evidence (BOE) submission packet will reduce the challenges of using an uncertified CSP; plan accordingly if considering moving part or all the business' operations into the "cloud."

A Shared Responsibility Model

In migrating workloads to the cloud, the CSP will provide compute, bandwidth, and storage capabilities. It is important that the CSP provide the proper security mechanisms, such as firewalls, two-factor authentication, and whitelisting access controls. As discussed previously, the SO (customer) is overall accountable for including security requirements in any contracts, Request for Proposals (RFP), Statements of Work (SOW) (explicit requirements) or Statements of Objectives (targeted requirements), and Task Orders.

For example, an Infrastructure as a Service (IaaS), where the 'infrastructure' is provided by a CSP, the SO is accountable for the security of the following, at a minimum, while the CSP may or may not be responsible based upon the terms of the specified CSLA and overall contract terms. These may include, for example, updating, patching, or maintaining the following at prescribed or ad hoc periods based upon the terms of the CSLA:

- **Operating Systems (OS)**
- **Applications and Databases**
- **Virtual Machines (VM)**
- **Credentials to include Public and Private Keys**
- **Adhering to DOD policies and configurations, i.e., Security Technical Implementation Guides (STIG)**
- **Vulnerability Compliance Reporting**
- **Data in Transit (DIT)/Data at Rest (DAR) Encryption**

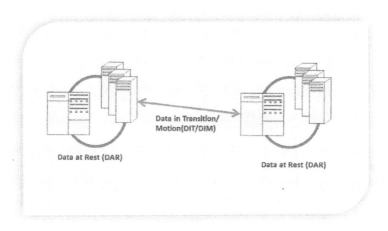

Data at Rest (DAR) versus Data in Transit/Motion (DIT/DIM) Conceptual Diagram

Additionally, the Office of Management and Budget (OMB) Directive M-15-131 (2015) "requires all publicly accessible Federal websites and web services only provide service through a secure connection." The SO is required to encrypt the DIT and DAR specific to its IT system and its defined security boundary. With regards to encryption, a US-based SO will utilize FIPS 140-2 compliant products as identified below. The website (https://csrc.nist.gov/projects/cryptographic-module-validation-program/validated-modules/search) should be used to determine whether the company or agency has a US-approved encryption solution.

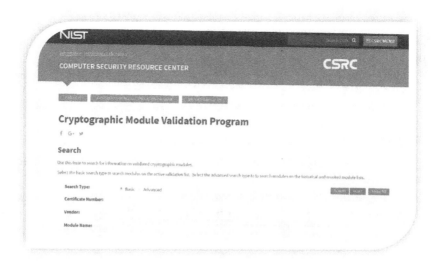

Cryptographic Module Validation Program Site

Below are examples and descriptions of several NIST-based *general* security controls that are designed to address Data in Transit (DIT) and Data at Rest (DAR) cryptographic protection responsibilities. They include:

"The protection of the authenticity of communications sessions"

> *This generalized National Institute of Standards and Technology (NIST) control addresses communications' protection and establishes confidence that the session is authentic; it ensures the identity of the individual and the information being transmitted. Authenticity protection includes, for example, protecting against session hijacking or insertion of false information. (NIST 800-171, Control: 3.13.15).*

This can be resolved by some form, hard or soft token Multi-Factor (MFA) or Two-factor authentication (2FA) solution. It ensures the identity and FIPS 140-2 encryption standard to prevent data intrusion and manipulation.

"Control the flow of sensitive data flowing and ensuring via approved authorization"

Companies, for example, typically use **flow control** policies and technologies to manage the movement of CUI/CDI (sensitive data) throughout the IT architecture; flow control is based on the types of information and the regulatory requirements that designate the type and levels of protection to include encryption.

In terms of procedural updates, discussion of the policy documents should address several areas of concern: 1) That only authorized personnel within the company with the requisite need-to-know are provided access; 2) appropriate security measures are in place to include encryption while Data is in Transit (DIT); 3) what are the procedures for handling internal employees who violate these company rules?; and, 4) how does the company alert the government if there is external intrusion (hackers) to its IT infrastructure and its NIST 800-171 data sets such as CUI and CDI?

Flow control could also be better demonstrated to a government assessor in terms of a technical solution. This can be demonstrated by using encryption for DIT and Data at Rest (DAR). These encryption requirements can be found in both NIST 800-171 and NIST 800-53. They necessitate technical solutions and use of Federal Information Processing Standards (FIPS) 140-2 compliant encryption solutions. (NIST 800-171, Control: 3.1.3).

To be successful, the CSC must clearly know which security controls their responsibility is, and which are those of the CSP. The CSLA forms the basis of documenting this information as part of an overall cybersecurity plan. Additionally, the CSP needs to have a document, spreadsheet, etc., that accounts for all controls, and where they reside between the CSC and CSP to meet outside auditing requirements. The shared responsibility model is ideal and helps to shift some of the functionality and especially security requirements to a competent CSP.

SECTION 2: SECURITY AND AVAILABILITY CHALLENGES

Assessment and Authorization (A&A)

The SO **must** apply Security Technical Implementation Guides (STIG) based upon the direction of the DOD—especially if supporting an existing DOD contract. Where the supported agency is not the DOD, it is still strongly recommended that companies, businesses, and agencies actively employ STIGs in their system hardening efforts. STIGs are formulated for major hardware and software components and are the foundation of policy and configuration settings that will afford the highest levels of security based upon the DOD as the *de jure* standard for the US government.

Since the major STIGs are typically restricted to current military, government, and contract employees, a less-stringent and more accessible option is the "National Checklist Program Repository." It provides "...publicly available security checklists (or benchmarks) that provide detailed low-level guidance on setting the security configuration of operating systems and applications." This supports both manual and automated configuration checks for hardware and software components to include such major manufacturers as Cisco, Apple, Microsoft, Apache, Oracle, etc. Leveraging and implementing these tools will require IT or cybersecurity professionals experienced in administering these tools. Furthermore, the information is provided at no-cost to the public. The site can be found at: https://nvd.nist.gov/ncp/repository.

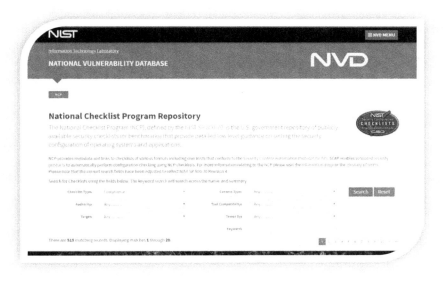

National Checklist Program Repository

The SO should also mandate this contractually with their respective CSP and should seek a third-party auditing agency to confirm these settings have been implemented. Federal FEDRAMP community calls these entities Third-Party Assessment Organizations (3PAO). While a CSP may be allowed to **"self-assess"** and report that its STIG activities are complete, it is still the SO who is accountable for any failures due to improper or incomplete STIG implementation. It is *strongly* recommended that the SO obtain qualified 3PAO FEDRAMP/NIST-based security auditors to ensure the CSP is in full compliance during initial deployment to the cloud.

The costs, while not recommended, of allowing the CSP to conduct its own self-assessment is about $20,000 to $40,000. The full costs if using an independent 3PAO may be as much as $300,000. More typically, the cost will be in the s $150,000 to $200,000 range. Our strongest advice is **_NOT_** to allow the CSP to assess its own readiness; the costs paid up-front will ensure reduced liability if the companies data is lost, compromised or destroyed.

The SO must also obtain an Interim Authority to Operate (IATO) or Authority to Operate (ATO) for mission information systems hosted in the cloud. The provisional authorizations are specific to the CSP and may be leveraged by the assigned Authorizing Official[9] (AO)—usually a senior corporate officer who may also be the SO as part of the risk decision process. All systems must have an ATO prior to connecting to other networks to include the SO's local IT environment as well as the CSP; the CSP, via the CSLA, will be responsible for all controls designated as part of the service agreement process.

The same process is used to accredit systems hosted, for example, in a DOD Data Center. This includes any virtualized environments especially specific to a cloud architecture. In 2014, the DOD abandoned the DOD-unique DoD Information Assurance Certification and Accreditation Process (DIACAP) and moved to the more global federal implementation of the DOD RMF. NIST created RMF and has become the *de facto* standard for the US federal government for cybersecurity.

Proof of Cybersecurity Posture

Typically, the minimum requirement to demonstrate control implementation is through **documentation**. Another term that is used is an **artifact**. An artifact is any representation to an independent third-party assessor that shows compliance with specific security controls. It is a major part of the proof that a SO would provide to a CO or independent security auditor.

The common term for the collection of all applications and supporting artifacts is the BOE. These documents are not a major discussion topic within this book; however, they are important as the base documents for any accreditation submission. The reader may have to

---

[9] The Authorizing Official (AO) is the most senior person in the cybersecurity chain of command and ultimately accepts or rejects the SO documented and reviewed submission whether the system is in full-compliance with applicable cybersecurity law, regulations or standards; the AO accepts all risk for the system based upon the SO's development of an IT-based system.

review with their CSP, their current BOE specific to these artifacts. The reason for such a review is to determine the current state of the cybersecurity posture of the CSP. These documents will help the SO determine the range of capabilities and shortfalls of the CSP, and how to better negotiate terms and costs based upon the completeness and accuracy of these core documents. The major items required for a BOE includes three major items:

1. **Company Policy or Procedure.** Essentially it is any written and formally approved direction provided to internal employees and subcontractors that are enforceable under US labor laws and Human Resource direction. It is recommended that such a policy or procedure artifact be a singular collection of how the company addresses each of the security controls.

2. **System Security Plan (SSP).** This is a standard cybersecurity document. It describes the company's overall IT infrastructure to include hardware and software lists.

A free 36-minute introduction to the SSP is currently available on Udemy.com at https://www.udemy.com/system-security-plan-ssp-for-nist-800-171-compliance/.

---

3. **Plans of Action and Milestones (POAM).** A POAM describes any control that cannot be fixed or can demonstrate its full compliance. It provides an opportunity to delay addressing a difficult to implement technical solution or because cost may be prohibitive. POAMs should always have an expected completion date and defined interim milestones that describes the actions leading to a full resolution or implementation of the control. *POAMs typically should not be for more than a year, however, an extension multiple times is reasonable if unable to meet the control.*

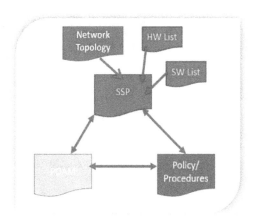

The Major Artifacts Required by the Federal Government under NIST 800-171

"Bastion" Considerations and "Defense in Depth"

When implementing a cloud environment, the SO should utilize the "Defense in Depth" principle for cybersecurity protection of corporate or agency sensitive data. One of the least expensive security system solution is a "Bastion Host." The Committee on National Security Systems (CNSS) Instruction No. 400920, defines a Bastion Host as "a special purpose computer on a network specifically designed and configured to withstand attacks." The computer generally hosts a single application, for example a proxy server, and all other services are removed or limited to reduce the threat to the computer.

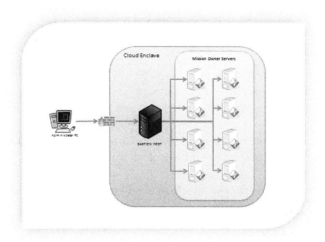

Basic Bastion Host Architecture

A cloud-based Bastion Host's sole purpose is to provide administrative access to other Virtual Machines (VM). It is recommended that a server with 1 – 2 CPUs and 4 GB of memory is available. When not required, a Bastion Host should be turned off. If using Active Directory and establishing a domain, recommend that the Bastion Host is NOT a member of the domain. This prevents if coincidentally the Bastion Host is compromised, the attacker will not have direct access to the domain.

Defense in Depth, also called "layered defense," may include, such additional protections to a company or agency's IT assets:

- Physical protection (e.g., security fencing, alarms, badging systems, biometric controls, guards)
- Perimeter (e.g., firewalls, Intrusion Detection Systems (IDS), Intrusion Prevention Systems[10] (IPS), "Trusted Internet Connections")
- Data (e.g., Data Loss Prevention (DLP) programs, access controls, auditing)
- Application/Executables (e.g., **whitelisting** of authorized software, **blacklisting** blocking specified programs). (See the NIST 800-171 control SI 3.14.2 below).

---

[10] Most IPS include IDS capabilities; the objective is if employed, an IPS will both "detect" and "prevent" the intrusion.

SYSTEM AND INFORMATION INTEGRITY (SI) CONTROL:
3.14.2: Provide protection from malicious code at appropriate locations within organizational information systems.

Protecting the network from malicious code is typically through both active anti-virus and malware protection applications or services. Ensure if additional protections provided by the Internet Service Provider (ISP) is included in any artifact submission included within a CSLA.

Any additional protections could also be provided by "smart" firewalls, routers, and switches. Certain commercial devices provide extra defenses.

Smart Firewalls. Smart firewalls include whitelisting and blacklisting protections.

- **Whitelisting** can be used only to allow authorized outside users on an internal Access Control List (ACL). The ACL needs to be managed actively to ensure that legitimate organizations can communicate through the businesses' firewall. The external interested business or organization can still communicate with the business for some services like the company web site and email system that resides in what is termed the Demilitarized Zone (DMZ). Whitelisting is typically implemented at the firewall.

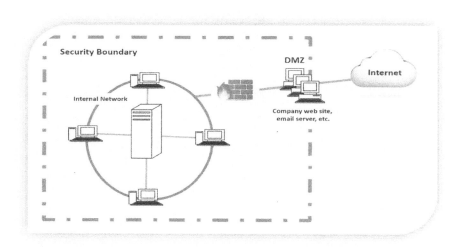

Basic Company Network View

- **Blacklisting** is used to block known "bad guys." There are companies and the government that can provide lists of known malicious sites based upon their Internet address. Blacklists require continuous management to be most effective.

Either of these solutions alone are not guaranteed to fully protect a network from outside threats, and certainly won't prevent an insider threat with full rights and accesses. While they afford additional means to slow hackers and nation-state intruders, they are not total solutions. The government, and much of the cybersecurity community, strongly support the principle of **Defense in Depth (DID)** where other technological solutions help to reinforce the protections because of security programming flaws and weaknesses.

The Principle of Defense in Depth

DID relies upon multiple layers of technical and administrative controls and are designed to further thwart threats to a company or agency's network. Flaws inadvertently created by software developers create constant opportunities for hackers exploiting modern IT architectures. DID is designed to be a holistic solution to better mitigate and reduce risk.

High "Availability" Focus

Regardless of the CSP, there are specific mechanisms to achieve high availability. The SO must plan a robust and secure architecture that affords all required functionalities critical to the operation of the business or agency. It is vital to understand that cybersecurity, and more specifically the RMF, takes into consideration three key security objectives for information and information systems. They are **Confidentiality** (**C**), **Integrity** (**I**), and **Availability** (**A**). Each of the three objectives are rated as either High (H), Moderate (M) or Low (L) for each Information System. An approach for the protection and availability of the system will differ based on the level designated. A H-H-M system requires greater protections, but only requires moderate availability; the third position is for Availability. A system with L-L-H, such as a banking system, requires a very high availability based upon its need to meet a very demanding customer base.

Specific to issues that may impact a CSP's Availability capabilities typically can be identified by five different systemic failures. All should be considered in determination of CSLA terms impacting availability of services in a cloud infrastructure.

1. *Application Failure*: To illustrate, a SharePoint Server is operating, and the web server service fails.
   - One solution is to build in fault tolerance into the application and define behaviors for application or system errors. This includes information that must be logged in the error logs.

2. *Server Failure* (including misconfiguration):
   - One solution involves spreading the workload across multiple servers and utilizing a **load balancer**. Additionally, the SO must work with their stakeholders in determining the appropriate level of data replication to avoid the impact of a server failure and the loss of access to the data temporarily or permanently.

3. *Data Center Failure* (including zone failure):
   - Most CSPs maintain alternate sites replicating data across their infrastructure. This is described as using **multiple zones** [data in another data center].
   - Another solution is to separate the load into different zones.

4. *Network Failure*: This may include general network congestion by other customers using the CSP.

- o The impact to the SO and his customers must be considered, and refunds or credits may be appropriate under a negotiated CSLA.
- o If caused by local Internet Service Provider (ISP) providing the connectivity to the CSP this may be an issue for the SO under the ISP SLA vice the CSP CSLA.

5. *Whole Cloud Failure*:
   - o The impact to the SO must be considered, and refunds or credits should be appropriate under a negotiated CSLA.

While availability is certainly key to any business, it must balance its priorities to include especially security. The CSP is typically measured most significantly against the factor of availability of services. A fine balance must be maintained and recognized by the CSC in terms of the overall CSLA and its associated SLO. The CSC must always be mindful that sometimes a loss of availability may be triggered by security or related integrity issues. The suggestion here for the CSC is to not overly penalize a CSP when an overriding issue of security, such as an unauthorized intrusion by hackers, etc., reduces the availability of services. The CSP should be aware that a temporary reduction in this area may be warranted to reduce damage, and better protect the CSP's overall interests operating in a cloud environment safely and securely.

SECTION 3: SERVICE LEVEL OBJECTIVE (SLO) CANDIDATES AND THEIR DESCRIPTIONS

Security Service Level Objectives (SSLO)

Specifying measurable security level objectives in CSLAs is useful to improve both assurance and transparency. Currently, it allows for establishing common terminology specific to the controls required by the customer and available by the CSP. Under a negotiated model, there is greater assurance for the customer to manage cloud security from two perspectives. They are:

1. **The security level being offered by a CSP**

2. **The security level requested by a CSC**

The approach used in this section consists of analyzing security controls from well-known frameworks into one or more security SLOs. These SLOs can be either quantitative or qualitative. This section focuses on the definitions of possible security SLOs. Eight categories are provided with one or more SLOs.

The categories are representative of important security requirements. However, not all security requirement categories are reflected below, as relevant SLOs may not exist for each of them. For example, resilience, business continuity, and disaster recovery are important aspects of security, specific controls and measures are usually put in place by CSPs, but no SLO has been derived for these security aspects.

For each category, the SLOs are meant to provide more quantitative and qualitative information relevant to a specific control, in addition to what is usually assessed in the context of an audit for a certification. It should be noted that the list of SLOs is not meant to be considered as exhaustive and that the SLOs proposed are not meant to be considered as applicable in all individual cases. The applicability of a SLO can depend on the type of service offered (in terms of both of service functionality and service model) and pricing (e.g., free service, paid, premium). It is important to understand that some of the SLOs relevant to security also have relevance in the areas of Data Management, Performance and Data Privacy and those SLOs are found in those sections.

Service Reliability

Service reliability is the property of a cloud service to perform its function correctly and without failure, typically over some period. Reliability also covers the capability of the cloud service to deal with failures and to avoid loss of service or loss of data in the face of such failures. This category is usually related to the security controls implementing business continuity management and disaster recovery in frameworks, for example, NIST 800-53 (RMF) and ISO/IEC 27002. Authorized downtime specific to all standard CSP maintenance should be commonly accepted in the CSLA since these are periods where, for example, critical security and application patches can be applied during required uninterrupted times to execute software and firmware "pushes." These are typical and standard configuration management updates directly applicable to all standard cybersecurity protection frameworks and best practices.

Reliability is sometimes described as "certification", but the target for reliability needs to be stated so that the cloud service customer can assess whether the cloud service meets their business requirements. Some data management SLOs can also be relevant to reliability – see section "Data Management SLOs".

SLO	SLO Description
Level of Redundancy	Describes the level of redundancy of the cloud service supply chain. It considers the percentage (%) of the components or service that have a fail-over mechanism. Redundancy varies also based upon the type of cloud service provided (e.g., IaaS versus SaaS).
Service Reliability	Describes the ability of the CSP to perform its function correctly and without failure over some specified period (time).

Authentication & Authorization (AA)

Authentication and Authorization (AA) is the verification of the claimed identity of an entity (typically for cloud computing the entity is a cloud service user). (Please note that this is difference than AA which applies to authorization to operates and connect to an active network while AA applies to verification of one's identity within an operational network). It is the process of verifying that an entity has permission to access and use a resource based upon a predefined user privilege level. AA are key elements of information security which applies to the use of cloud services.

Certification generally validates AA mechanisms are established, but do not in general provide details of how those mechanisms are provided. It is important as an accountable SO that such means are known and provided.

SLO	SLO Description
User Authentication and Identity Assurance Level	Measures the Level of Assurance (LOA) of the mechanism used to authenticate a user accessing a resource. The LOA can be based on relevant standards like NIST SP 800-63 (Electronic Authentication Guidelines), ISO/IEC 29115 (Entity Authentication Assurance Framework) or the Kantara Initiative's Identity Assurance Framework (IAF).
Authentication	Specifies the available authentication mechanisms supported by the CSP on its offered cloud services. In some cases, the customer might need to analyze along with the CSP, those mechanisms allowing interoperability among their authentication schemes (e.g., cross-certification in the case of digital certificate-based authentication).
Mean Time Required to Revoke User Access	The average time required to revoke users' access to the cloud service on request over a specified period.
User Access Storage Protection	Describes the mechanisms used to protect cloud service user access credentials
Third Party Authentication Support	Specifies whether third party authentication is supported by the cloud service and defines which technologies can be used for third party authentication. This SLO complements the previously defined "Authentication" SLO and is the basis for interoperable authentication/identity management solutions between customer and providers.

Cryptography (Encryption)

Cryptography is a discipline which includes the principles, means and methods for the data transformation that obscures or hides the information content. It prevents undetected modifications and prevents its unauthorized use.

While many certification approaches require the use of data encryption in a variety of circumstances there are many encryption methods in use and they vary in their strength and cost to implement. It is necessary for the CSLA to describe specifics relating to encryption methods for the CSC to evaluate a cloud service fully since few certifications require the use of specific encryption methods.

SLO	SLO Description
Cryptographic Brute Force Resistance	Expresses the strength of a cryptographic protection applied to a resource based on its key length, for example using the ECRYPT II security level recommendations or the FIPS security levels for encryption. Instead of using key lengths alone, which are not always directly comparable from one algorithm to another, this normalizing scale allows comparison of the strengths of different types of cryptographic algorithms.
Key Access Control Policy	Describes how strongly a cryptographic key is protected from access, when it is used to provide security to the cloud service (or assets within the cloud service).
Cryptographic Hardware Module Protection Level	Describes the level of protection that is afforded to cryptographic operations in the cloud service using cryptographic hardware modules.

Security Incident Management and Reporting

An information security incident is a single or a series of unwanted or unexpected information security events that have a significant probability of compromising business operations and threatening information security. Information security incident management are the processes for detecting, reporting, assessing, responding to, dealing with, and learning from information security incidents.

How information security incidents are handled by a CSP is of great concern to cloud service customers, since an information security incident relating to the cloud service is also an information security incident for the CSC. In the discussion earlier of NIST 800-171 and its framework, it was noted that if the CSC is providing services to the DOD, it must report that incident to the government typically within 72 hours. Incident response is also critical to the CSC where it provides services to other customers to include the US federal government concerned about the security posture of its contractor workforce.

Incident Response primarily requires a plan, an identification of who or what agency is notified when a breach has occurred and testing of the plan over time. This control requires the development of an Incident Response Plan (IRP).

EVENT → INCIDENT
(less defined/initial occurrence) → (defined/confirmed/high impact)

Incident Response Spectrum

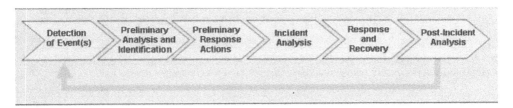

DOD Cyber Incident Life Cycle. This diagram from the DOD is helpful in assisting a company's approach to IR activities with and by the CSP and its role. It will better assist in coordination with government cybersecurity incident response organizations. Recognizing this as either an "event" (not necessarily a negative occurrence) versus an "incident" is an internal determination by the company's leadership in coordination with the CSP. An incident specifically requires alerting the CSC as soon as the intrusion is ***recognized***.

Typically, **events** may not need to be reported based on the expansive impacts and workloads to government cybersecurity response organizations. In the case of **incidents**, the standard is 72-hours; however, the recommendation is *as soon as possible* due to the potential impacts beyond the company's own IT infrastructure and its use of a cloud service. It can pose a serious direct threat to other supported customers by the CSC to include the government.

SLO	SLO Description
Percentage of Timely Incident Reports	Describes the defined incidents to the cloud service which are reported to the customer in a timely fashion. This is represented as a percentage by the number of defined incidents reported within a predefined time limit after discovery, over the total number of defined incidents to the cloud service which are reported within a predefined period (i.e. month, week, year, etc.).
Percentage of Timely Incident Responses	Describes the defined incidents that are assessed and acknowledged by the cloud service provider in a timely fashion. This is represented as a percentage by the number of defined incidents assessed and acknowledged by the cloud service provider within a predefined time limit after discovery, over the total number of defined incidents to the cloud service within a predefined period. (i.e. month, week, year, etc.).
Percentage of Timely Incident Resolutions	Describes the percentage of defined incidents against the cloud service that are resolved within a predefined time limit after discovery.

Logging and Monitoring

Logging is the recording of data related to the operation and use of a cloud service. **Monitoring** means determining the status of one or more parameters of a cloud service. Logging and monitoring are ordinarily the responsibility of the CSP.

Log file entries are important to cloud service customers when analyzing incidents such as security breaches and service failures as well as in monitoring the customer's daily use of the service. It is necessary for there to be service level objective relating to logging and monitoring to fully describe the cloud service and its related capabilities.

SLO	SLO Description
Logging Parameters	Describes the parameters that are captured in the cloud service log files.
Log Access Availability	Describes what log file entries the cloud service customer has access to.

Logs Retention Period	Describes the period during which logs are available for analysis (e.g. the period that log files are available for use by the cloud service customer).

Security Auditing

Auditing is the systematic, **independent** and documented process for obtaining audit evidence about a cloud service and evaluating it **objectively** to determine the extent to which the audit criteria are fulfilled. The audit evidence and criteria are usually determined by the audit, certification, but more specifically through the RMF security control selection process. (See the RMF process below.)

Risk Management Framework (RMF) Lifecycle
SOURCE: https://csrc.nist.gov/Projects/Risk-Management/Risk-Management-Framework-(RMF)-Overview

Audits are a means by which the CSP may offer evidence that a cloud service meets criteria of interest to the CSC; however, self-assessment by these means while accepted under RMF, they are highly questioned by professionals within the cybersecurity assessment community. While the objective is to provide trust into the cloud service industry, the principle of **separation of duties** is directly violated by this this approach. It poses many challenges for further conflict of interest concerns when the CSP is "scoring his own" commercial venture.

SLO	SLO Description
Certifications Applicable[11]	Refers to a list of certifications held by the cloud service provider for a cloud service, including the certifying body, the expiration date of each certification and the renewal period.

Vulnerability Management

A vulnerability is a weakness in an information system, system security procedures, internal controls, or implementation that could be exploited or triggered by a threat. Management of vulnerabilities means that information about technical vulnerabilities of information systems being used should be obtained in a timely fashion, the organization's exposure to such vulnerabilities evaluated and appropriate measures taken to address the associated risk.

Many of the information systems associated with a cloud service belong to the cloud service provider with the result that the cloud service customer is dependent on the provider for appropriate and timely management of vulnerabilities of those systems. SLOs for vulnerability management provide transparency for the customer.

SLO	SLO Description
Percentage of Timely Vulnerability Corrections	Describes the number of vulnerability corrections performed by the cloud service provider and is represented as a percentage by the number of vulnerability corrections performed within a predefined time limit, over the total number of vulnerability corrections to the cloud service which are reported within a predefined period (i.e. month, week, year, etc.).
Percentage of Timely Vulnerability Reports	Describes the number of vulnerability reports by the cloud service provider to the cloud service customer and is represented as a percentage by the number of vulnerability reports within a predefined time limit, over the total number of vulnerability reports to the cloud service which are reported within a predefined period (i.e. month, week, year, etc.).
Reports of Vulnerability Corrections	Is a description of the mechanism by which the CSP informs the customer of vulnerability corrections applied to the provider's systems to include frequency of reports.

---

[11] "Certifications" are typically provided by a third-party organization and is the basis for many of the compliance requirements a CSP should be assessed against. The cloud customer should question any "self-assessed" certification, but this is not necessarily grounds to not accept a CSP.

Governance

Governance is a system by which cloud service is directed and controlled. The main area of concern is the way in which changes and updates to a cloud service are managed whether the "change request" originates with the cloud service customer or originates with the CSP. This is specific to the Configuration Management (CM) controls required under, for example, NIST 800-53 and 800-171, respectively. Governance establishes the policies and procedures to effectively manage and monitor change during the life of a system or network.

The following SLO controls were identified specifically from NIST 800-171 revision 1[12], ***Protecting Unclassified Information in Nonfederal Information Systems and Organizations***, and should only be considered representation of potential security controls traceable to a SLO. Any SLO selection will be based upon the security controls of determine cybersecurity standard.

SLO	SLO Description
Baseline Configuration Control	(Control 3.4.1). Establish and maintain baseline configurations and inventories of organizational information systems (including hardware, software, firmware, and documentation) throughout the respective system development life cycles. This should be an ongoing effort where the CSP advises of their configuration changes that may impact the CSC's operations, or may include extended services by the CSP to maintain documentation management of behalf of the CSC
Maintain an Audit Change Information System	(Control 3.4.3). Track, review, approve/disapprove, and audit changes to information systems. This may include CSP changes that are reported on a recurring basis, or a fee for service extension to the CSLA.
Percentage of Timely Cloud Service Change Notifications	(Control 3.4.4). Analyze the security impact of changes prior to implementation. The CSP will conduct and document a Security Impact Assessment (SIA) for all non-standard changes (e.g., security and application update patches). This should address whether the changes are: 1) "security relevant" [13]," and 2) do not adversely impact the CSC by impacting its operational state.

---

[12] There are 9 potential CM security controls in NIST 800-171 that may be negotiated with a potential CSP.

[13] "Any change to a system's configuration, environment, information content, functionality, or users which has the potential to change the risk imposed upon its continued operations." Source: CNSSI 4009-2015

Service Changes

Cloud services may change. Examples of service changes include changes to functionality, service interfaces or application of software updates. It may be reflected in the CSLA or in another contractual document. Cloud service customers should require a reasonable notification period before changes occur. Such changes may adversely impact the business or agency. Notifications prepare CSCs and their IT support staffs to be better prepared for adverse impacts to customers and employees. It can prepare organizations of possible downtimes.

SLO	SLO Description
Cloud Service Change	Describes the type of change (such as CSLA change or functional change)
Reporting Notifications	mechanism and period for the cloud service provider to notify cloud service customers of planned changes to the cloud service.
Percentage of Timely Cloud Service Change Notifications	The number of change notifications made within a specified period over the total number of change notifications. Can be expressed as a percentage.

Performance Service Level Objectives

This section covers the common SLOs that relate to the performance of the cloud service and of related aspects of interfaces between the CSC and CSP. This set of SLOs is not an exhaustive list but establishes a foundation for the SO and the IT support staff to be better engaged with the CSP; not all SLOs may be fully applicable to a specified cloud service.

Availability

"Availability is the accessibility and usability upon demand by an authorized entity."

Availability is usually covered by certification at a general level. Availability is a key SLO since it describes whether the cloud service can be used. It also specifies numeric values in terms of time or percentage of availability. These units of measure support meaningful statements that are provides a baseline of measure that supports measurements and verification of the QOS provided. It is valuable that the CSLA provide clear information on these aspects of service availability.

The question of what "usable" means is a complex. It depends on the cloud service and its ability to provide some or all the services required by the CSC. Additionally, the service may be available, but respond with error filled responses that do not meet the CSLA's specified SLO. Conversely, a service may be available but perform so poorly that its information is useless to the CSC.

SLO	SLO Description
Level of Uptime (Often termed "availability")	Describes the time in a defined period the service was available, over the total possible available time. Expressed as a percentage. Some cloud services specify that the service will be unavailable for specified periods for maintenance. It is common for the stated level of uptime to exclude these maintenance periods. In this case Uptime = Total Possible Available Time − (Total Downtime − Maintenance Downtime).
Percentage of Successful Requests	Describes the number of requests processed by the service without an error over the total number of submitted requests. Expressed as a percentage.

Percentage of timely service provisioning requests	Describes the number of service provisioning requests completed within a defined time over the total number of service provisioning requests, expressed as a percentage. Provisioning of cloud services may vary greatly depending on the type of service being considered – from storage provisioning to user account provisioning. It is thus expected that this SLO will need to be tailored to the service being considered.

Response Time

Response time is the time interval between a customer-initiated event (stimulus) and a CSP-initiated event in response to that stimulus. Response time SLOs can vary depending on the point at which the customer's stimulus is measured. For example, the measurement may start when the customer initiates the stimulus on a device, or it may start from the point when the request from the customer arrives at the cloud service provider's endpoint.

Response time can be a highly significant aspect of the user experience. Response times that are greater than some established threshold is regarded as unacceptable and may cause the cloud service to become unusable. Rarely are response times dealt with directly by certifications and furthermore response times can vary depending on the nature of the request concerned or the type of the service being considered.

A factor that needs to be considered is that many cloud services support multiple operations and it is likely that the response time will differ for the different operations; response times need to clearly state which operations are being supported and what level of support is required via the CSLA.

SLO	SLO Description
Average Response Time	Refers to the statistical means over a set of cloud service response time observations for a form of request.
Maximum Response Time	Refers to the maximum response time target for a given form of request.

Capacity

Capacity is the maximum amount of some property of a cloud service that may include number of simultaneous users, storage, load balancing, Denial of Service (DOS) defensive capabilities, etc. It is often an important value for cloud customers to know when using a cloud service. The relevant properties vary depending on the capabilities offered by the cloud service and it is often the case that differing capacities are relevant for a given cloud service specific to the types and kinds of functionality is being sought.

Capacities are rarely the subject of certification and must be stated clearly in the CSLA. Capacity SLOs refer to the capacities as determined by an individual cloud service customer and may or may not reflect the overall capacities supported by the CSP. The customer can change the capacity limits for their cloud service by requesting a change in their subscription and associated fees.

SLO	SLO Description
Number of Simultaneous Connections	Refers to the maximum number of separate connections to the cloud service at one time.
Number of Simultaneous Cloud Service Users	Refers to a target for the maximum number of separate cloud service customer users that can be using the cloud service at one time.
Maximum Resource Capacity	Refers to the maximum amount of a given resource available to an instance of the cloud service for a cloud service customer. Example resources include data storage, memory, number of CPU cores.
Service Throughput	Refers to the minimum number of specified requests that can be processed by the cloud service in a stated time. (e.g., requests per minute).

Capability Indicators

Capability indicators are SLOs which afford specific functionality relating to the cloud service. They can be essential to the use of the cloud service from the perspective of the cloud service customer.

SLO	SLO Description
External Connectivity	Specifies Capabilities of the cloud service to connect to systems and services which are external to the cloud service. The systems and services involved may be other cloud services or they may be outside a cloud computing environment (e.g. in-house customer systems, other networks that are not cloud-based).

Support

Support is the interface approaches (e.g., telephonic, self-service, etc.) available by the CSP to address issues and queries raised by the CSC. Support capabilities may be required by certification, but the details are typically not covered by certification and must instead be described by appropriate SLOs.

SLO	SLO Description
Support Hours	Specifies the hours during which the CSP provides a cloud service customer support and accepts inquiries and requests from customers.
Support Responsiveness	Specifies the maximum time the CSP will take to acknowledge a cloud customer inquiry or request. It is typical for responsiveness to vary depending on a severity level (Tier 1 [basic], Tier 2 [intermediate], and Tier 3 [advanced/Original Equipment Manufacturer (OEM)-level]. Times should be apportioned by the severity level.
Resolution Time	Refers to the target resolution time for customer requests. This is the amount of time used to complete a user request. This target time can vary depending on the severity level of the customer request.

Reversibility and the Termination Process

The termination process occurs when a cloud service customer or a CSP elect to terminate the agreement that includes the terms of a CSLA. The termination process includes a series of steps which enables the customer to retrieve their data within a stated period before the CSP deletes the data include backup copies and prior or archived versions of files and databases. A CSP can potentially delete or aggregate any data which may include "derived data"[14] that relates to the customers' data and their use of the cloud service. Certification requires a very well-defined termination process.

SLO	SLO Description
Data Retrieval Period	Specifies the length of time in which the customer can retrieve a copy of their data to include all files, databases, and archive records that may or may not include audit logs.[15]
Data Retention Period	Refers to the length of time which the CSP will retain backup copies of the customer data during the termination process in case of problems with the retrieval process, for future legal or law enforcement purposes. This period may be subject to legal or regulatory requirements which can place lower or upper bounds on the length of time that the provider can retain copies of customer data.
Residual Data Retention	Refers to a description of any data relating to the cloud service customer which is retained after the end of the termination process. This is typically cloud service derived data which may be to regulatory controls.

---

[14] "Derived data" may include "external" data related which may include e.g., recipients, senders, audit log retention, etc. Such data may be covered under existing or future international and national laws and regulations.
[15] An audit log and associated files should be requested to determine whether there has been any unauthorized access during the termination period. While not typical, it most likely will incur additional costs.

Data Management Service Level Objectives

As companies transition to cloud computing, the traditional methods of securing and managing data are challenged by cloud-based architectures. Elasticity, multi-tenancy, new physical and logical architectures, and abstracted controls require new data security strategies. Managing data and information in the era of cloud computing can affect all organizations. It begins with managing internal data and cloud migrations and extends to securing information in diffuse, cross-organizational applications and services.

The data management SLOs presented in this section address important quantitative and qualitative indicators related to data life cycle management. They can be considered as complementary to existing and applicable security and data protection certifications offered by the CSP.

Data management SLOs are subdivided into four different top-level categories covering all aspects of the identified data life-cycle. Each category is subdivided into one or more SLOs that are applicable to that specific category. Not all SLOs may be relevant for each cloud service depending on the type of cloud service such as IaaS, PaaS or SaaS.

Data Classification

Data classification is a description of the classes of data which are associated with the cloud service. They typically include these three categories:

1.   Cloud Service Customer (CSC) Data
2.   Cloud Service Provider (CSP) Data
3.   Cloud Service Derived Data

Cloud customer data is a class of data objects under the control of the cloud service customer. Cloud service customer data includes data input into the cloud service by the cloud service customer and the results of the cloud service customer's use of the cloud service unless a Master Service Agreement (MSA), for example, specifically defines a different scope.

The following SLOs contain a specific list of data uses that can be applied to compare different CSP offerings. This information is usually difficult to deduce in specific and concrete ways from relevant security and data protection certifications. Customers should use this information to make an informed decision about their choice of CSP. This may include the CSP's listed "customer data uses" compliant with the customer's requirements?

SLO	SLO Description
Cloud Service Customer Data use by the provider	Describes stated policy for any intended use of cloud service customer data
Cloud Service Derived Data Use	Describes what derived data is created by the CSP from cloud service customer data, the intended uses for the derived data and what rights the cloud service customer should expect from access to any derived data

Cloud Service Customer Data Mirroring Backup & Restore

This SLO category addresses actual mechanisms used to guarantee that the customers' data is available and the restrictions regarding its release to the customer, law enforcement, and other third-party entities, etc. The mechanisms include the following SLO categories: 1) Data Mirroring, and 2) Backup and Restore.

Widely used security certification in this category include ISO/IEC 27002, and contains specific security controls that are implemented to avoid data loss. In many cases the information that can be extracted from those certifications rarely contain the basic measurements that can be used by the cloud customer to assess and monitor the activities of the CSP specific to this category of service.   These SLO categories address the following areas:

- The **timeliness** of the mirroring mechanisms which are directly related to the geographical location of the CSPs data centers.

- Details related to the **frequency** and **method** used by the CSP's backup and recovery mechanisms.

Proposed SLOs allow customers to fine-tune their risk assessments and business continuity procedures. They can further assist the cloud customer in identifying Recovery Point Objective (RPO) and Recovery Time Objective (RTO) metrics critical to developing quantitative SLOs adequate to meet the businesses recovery requirements.

RPO is the maximum allowable time between recovery points. RPO does not specify the amount of acceptable data loss and only provides for an acceptable period where recovery must occur in compliance with the CSLA. Furthermore, RPO affects data redundancy and backup. A small RPO suggests mirrored storage of both transient and persistent data while a larger window allows for a periodic backup approach. An RTO should determine the CSC's acceptable RPO for each cloud service used. It ensures that the CSP's own disaster recovery plans meet their objectives as well as those of the cloud customer.

RTO is the maximum amount of time a business process may be disrupted, for example, after a natural or man-made disaster[16] without suffering unacceptable business consequences. Cloud services can be critical components of business processes. Cloud service customers must determine the RTO for each of their cloud service dependent business processes and similarly determine whether both the CSP's and CSC's disaster recovery plans are sufficient.

SLO	SLO Description
Data Mirroring Latency	Refers to the difference between the time data is placed on primary storage and the time the same data is placed on mirrored storage.
Data Backup Method	Refers to a list of methods used to backup cloud data.
Data Backup Frequency	Refers to the period between complete backups of cloud service customer data.
Backup Retention Time	Refers to the period a given backup is available for use in data restoration.
Backup Generations	Refers to the number of backup generations available for use in data restoration.
Maximum Data Restoration time	Refers to the committed time taken to restore cloud service customer data from a backup.
Percentage of Successful Data Restorations	Refers to the committed success rate for data restorations, expressed as the number of data restorations performed for the customer without errors over the total number of data restorations, expressed as a percentage.

Data Lifecycle

The following list of SLOs is related to the efficiency and effectiveness of the provider's data lifecycle practices. The data lifecycle focuses on the practices and mechanisms for data handling and deletion.

---

[16] Depending on the geographic location, the CSLA may have to separate natural versus man-made disasters to include "act of God" and modern-day terrorist concerns.

Despite widely used security certifications schemes that address the topic of secure disposal,[17] the CSP-specific information related to the deletion and storage controls may be difficult to determine, but not impossible. The following list of SLOs provide information related with the assurance and timeliness associated with the deletion mechanism. These include quantitative SLOs associated with the reliability of the storage service (e.g., data retrievability and stored data durability). The cloud customer should be concerned about data retrieval after a deletion request has been executed based upon the SLO. Cloud service customers can use the following list of SLOs to determine, for example, their choice of available cloud storage mechanisms offered by the CSP.

SLO	SLO Description
Data Deletion Type	Describes the quality of data deletion, ranging from 'weak' deletion where only the reference to the data is removed, to 'strong' sanitization techniques to ensure that deleted data cannot be easily recovered[18].
Percentage of Timely Effective Deletions	Refers to the number of cloud service customer data deletion requests completed within a predefined time limit over the total number of deletion requests. Expressed in term of a percentage.
Percentage of Tested Storage Retrievability	Refers to the amount of cloud service customer data that has been verified to be retrievable during the measurement period after the data has been deleted.

Data Portability

The following list of SLOs is related to the CSP capabilities to export data so it may be further used by the customer in the event of contract termination. In related security controls frameworks and certifications, the implementation of data portability controls usually focuses on the specification of applicable CSP policies which may be difficult for cloud customers to extract the specific indicators related to:

1. Available Data Formats
2. Interfaces

---

[17] "Data Security & Information Lifecycle Management" in CSA's Cloud Controls Matrix

[18] For more information on this topic please refer to "NIST Special Publication 800-88: Guidelines for Media Sanitization".

3. Transfer Rates.

The following list of SLOs focuses on these three basic aspects of the CSP data portability features which can be used by the customer, for example, to negotiate the technical features associated with the provider's termination process.

SLO	SLO Description
Data Portability Format	Specifies the electronic format(s) in which cloud service customer data can be transferred to/accessed from the cloud service.
Data Portability Interface	Specifies the mechanisms which can be used to transfer cloud service customer data to and from the cloud service. This specification potentially includes the transport protocols, APIs or other mechanism that is supported.
Data Transfer Rate	Refers to the minimum rate at which cloud service customer data can be transferred to/from the cloud service using the mechanism(s) stated in the data interface.

Personal Data Protection Service Level Objectives

This chapter focuses on the definition of appropriate SLOs with reference to the cases where the CSP functions acts as a **"data processor"** on behalf of its customer (the **"data controller"**). Providers that act as data controllers or joint controllers[19] can still leverage this chapter. However, under this situation both parties must ensure compliance with their respective legal obligations that may occur from their own personal data controller roles.

We will concentrate on data protection measures that are suitable for being translated into SLOs, i.e. into objectives that must be achieved by the provider. Other data protection measures and obligations can be better managed through other instruments to include an adherence to a code of conduct, relevant contract and service agreement, applicable law, etc.

Codes of Conduct, Standards and Certification

The cloud customer, as data controller, must accept responsibility for abiding by the applicable data protection legislation. The cloud service customer has an obligation to assess the lawfulness of the processing of personal data in the cloud and to select a CSP that facilitates compliance with the applicable international and national laws specific to the protection of personal data. Personal data may include, but is not limited to, Personally Identifiable Information (PII), Personal Health Information (PHI), etc.

The CSP should make available all the necessary information and adhere to the "principle of transparency" as described in this section. Such information includes information that may assist in the assessment of the service such as the data protection codes of conduct, standards, or certification schemes that the CSP is required to legally meet on behalf of the CSC.

SLO	SLO Description
Applicable Data Protection Codes of Conduct, Standards, Certifications	A list of the data protection codes of conduct, standards and certification mechanisms that the service must meet. This may be provided by both the CSP and CSC subject to jurisdictional requirements and restrictions.

---

[19] Possibly occurring when the CSP is processing personal data for their own purposes outside of an explicit mandate from the customer and associated CSLA.

Purpose Specification

The principle of purpose specification and limitation requires that personal data must be collected for specified, explicit and legitimate purposes and not further processed in a way incompatible with those purposes[30]. Therefore, the purposes of the processing must be determined prior to the collection of personal data by the data controller who must also inform the CSP how that data is being handled and how the CSP may or may not be involved in its care and protection. [20]

When the data controller decides to process the data in the cloud it must ensure that personal data are not improperly or illegally released. The CSC may be able to seek automated CSP services that prevent the processing and release of such data outside the confines of the cloud service; it should also be able to prevent the customers subcontractors or third-party providers from violating these rules.

The CSP may not process personal data pursuant to the service agreement with its customer for its own purposes without the express permission of the customer. A CSP that processes customers' personal data *for its own purposes* outside of the CSLA, for example, conducting market or scientific analysis, to profile the CSC's data subjects, or to improve direct own marketing will be a violation of the CSLA, and should be grounds for immediate termination; any such situation should be discussed with legal representatives able to determine whether such a violation has occurred both with respect to the CSLA and applicable laws.

SLO	SLO Description
Processing Purposes	A list of processing purposes (if any) which are beyond those requested by the customer acting as a controller.

Data Minimization

The cloud service customer is responsible for ensuring that any personal data are erased by the provider and any supporting subcontractors once the data is determined that it is no longer required. It must adhere to the principle of data minimization that once the need or the use of the data occurs, it should be deleted by a process agreed to by the CSP and CSC in accordance with the CSLA.

---

[20] An example includes Data Loss Prevention (DLP) services. A CSP may be able to scan unencrypted files for personal data, social security numbers, etc., and block their transmittal by automated tools or devices.

Temporary data can be created during the operation of the cloud service; however, it may not be immediately deleted once its use expires. Periodic manual or automated checks should ensure that temporary data is effectively deleted after a predefined period.

The contract between the cloud service customer and the provider must include clear provisions for the erasure of personal data. Furthermore, since personal data may be maintained redundantly on different servers at various locations, it must ensure that both the CSP and CSC has identified these data stores and act in accordance with this requirement. Overall, the cloud customer is *ultimately* accountable for any criminal or civil violations of law. The procedure must further ensure each instance of the data is erased irretrievably (i.e., previous versions, temporary files, etc.).

SLO	SLO Description
Temporary Data Retention Period	The maximum period that temporary data is retained after identification that the temporary data is unused.
Cloud Service Customer Data Retention Period	The maximum period that cloud service customer data is retained before destruction by the CSP and after acknowledgment of a request to delete the data or termination of the contract.

Use, Retention and Disclosure Limits

In its capacity as data processor, the CSP will inform the customer within a reasonable time of any legally binding request for which the provider is compelled to disclose. This will typically occur by law enforcement or governmental authority requiring access to archived data for investigation unless otherwise prohibited. This situation may occur when authorities exercise specific powers to prohibit the CSP by legal prohibition to preserve the confidentiality of an investigation.

The following SLOs aim to quantify the disclosure to law enforcement authorities over a period and provide a means for a cloud customer to conduct market research in the pursuit of a CSP.

SLO	SLO Description
Number of Customer Data Law Enforcement Disclosures	Refers to the number of personal data disclosures to law enforcement authorities over a predefined period (applicable only if the communication of such disclosures is permitted by law).
Number of Personal Data Disclosure Notifications	Refers to the number of personal data disclosures to law enforcement authorities notified to the customer over a predefined period (applicable only if the communication of such disclosures is permitted by law).

Transparency and Notification

Only if the provider informs the customer about all relevant issues, the cloud service customer can fulfill its obligation as data controller to assess the lawfulness of the processing of personal data in the cloud. Moreover, the CSP shall make available the information that enables the customer to provide the data subjects with an adequate notice about the processing of their personal data as required by law; transparency in the cloud means it is necessary for the cloud service customer to be made aware of subcontractors contributing to the provisions of the respective CSLA.

Cloud service customer consent is necessary when a subcontractor relationship exists between the CSP as the "prime" contractor and any subcontractors. The cloud customer may object to changes in the list of subcontractors. To implement such provisions, the list of subcontractors must be made available to the customer especially if changes to subcontracting relationships change or are terminated.

The processing of certain special categories of data may require compliance with specific regulatory provisions which may not be covered by standards or certifications schemes of general application. The CSLA should specify possible special categories of data that the service is suitable for and further describe the types and kinds of protections to include levels of encryption for DAR and DIT. (See Page 31, "Data at Rest (DAR) versus Data in Transit/Motion (DIT/DIM) Conceptual Diagram").

SLO	SLO Description
List of tier 1 Subcontractors	Refers to the CSP's subcontractors involved in the processing of the cloud service customer's personal data.

Special Categories of Data	Refers to the list of the specific categories of personal data (if any), e.g. health-related or financial data or otherwise sensitive data, that the cloud service is suitable for processing, according to applicable standards or regulations.

Accountability

In data protection, accountability often takes a broad meaning and describes the ability of parties to demonstrate that they took appropriate steps to ensure that data protection principles have been implemented. IT accountability is particularly important for the investigation of personal data breaches. The cloud platform should provide reliable monitoring and logging mechanisms. CSPs should provide documentary evidence of appropriate and effective measures that are designed to deliver the outcomes of the data protection principles (e.g., procedures designed to ensure the identification of all data processing operations, response to access requests, designation of data protection officers, etc.). In addition, cloud service customers, as data controllers, should ensure that they are prepared to demonstrate the establishment of the necessary measures to the supervisory authorities to include law enforcement or government investigators.

The CSP must notify the cloud costumer in the event of a data breach that affects the customer's' data. The CSP shall implement a data breach management policy which specifies the procedures for establishing and communicating data breaches to both the customer as well as law enforcement especially when there is a potential violation of the law.

SLO	SLO Description
Personal Data Breach Policy	Describes the policy regarding data breaches.
Documentation	Refers to the list of the documents that the provider makes available to demonstrate compliance to data protection requirements and obligations (e.g. procedures to respond to access request, designation of data protection officers, certifications, etc.).

Geographical Location of Customer Data

Personal data processed in the cloud may be transferred. This may include by subcontractors to other countries whose laws do not guarantee an adequate level of data protection. This also implies that personal data may be disclosed to foreign law enforcement agency without a valid legal basis. To minimize these risks, the cloud service customer should verify that the provider guarantees lawfulness of cross-border data transfers, e.g. by framing such transfers with "Safe Harbor" arrangements, model clauses or binding corporate rules, as appropriate.

The cloud service customer shall be made aware of the location of data processed in the cloud especially if authorized data transfers occur to countries or jurisdictions not originally identified in the CSLA. The following SLOs represent the instruments based on which the cloud service customer can control the location of its data.

SLO	SLO Description
Data Geolocation List	Specifies the geographical location(s) where the cloud service customer data may be stored and processed.
Data Geolocation Selection	Specifies whether cloud service customer can choose a given geographical location for the storage of the cloud service customer data.

Intervenability

The CSC must **verify** that the CSP unilaterally cannot impose technical and organizational obstacles to the requirements. This would include situations when data is further processed by subcontractors. The contract between the CSC and CSP should stipulate that the provider is obliged to support the customer in facilitating the exercise and protection of its data. The CSP should be prevented from interfering with CSC's data rights and it be assured in a timely and efficient manner.

SLO	SLO Description
Access Request Response Time	Refers to the time within which the provider shall communicate the information necessary to allow the customer to respond to access requests by the data subjects

SECTION 4: A SERVICE LEVEL OBJECTIVES (SLO) CHECKLIST

How to Use the SLO Checklist Section

This section provides guidance and direction in developing critical SLO for a CSLA. However, it cannot determine every possibility or situation that would warrant less or more SLOs. This will be derived primarily by the cybersecurity framework chosen by the business or agency and applied, for example, NIST 800-53, NIST 800-171, etc. Every attempt has been made to provide a best practice representation but will require alignment with security controls that will be apportioned to the CSP where the company or agency has determined it cannot or will not be able to meet the control; most likely, the CSP will be better suited to manage the control.

The checklist is designed to establish **Pri**ority (1-3), whether the control will be the responsibility of the CSLA (**Y**[es]**?**), the **SLO**, and **Suggested Metric** write-up that may be used or not by the organization.[21] The priority should be determined by the following recommended factors:

- **PRIORITY   1**
  The control cannot be met by the organization and MUST be met to maintain its Authority to Operate (ATO); the cost for the service is not prohibitive and is part of the existing budget.

- **PRIORITY   2**
  The control may or may not be met by the organization and SHOULD be met to maintain its ATO. A POAM may also be used to address the control longer term. The cost for the service with the CSP is not prohibitive and is part of the existing budget.

- **PRIORITY   3**
  The control is optional and can easily be addressed by a documented and approved POAM, Risk Acceptance, or a Waiver. The cost for the service with the CSP may be prohibitive and may be met by the organization with its own organic capabilities. It may need to be budgeted in future years and may be captured in the form of a POAM as well.

---

[21] Any such binding documents should be reviewed by a legal professional prior specific to the laws and regulations of the particular jurisdiction.

Service Reliability

PRI	Y?	SLO	Suggested Metric
2		Level of Redundancy	*Upon a scheduled or unscheduled outage, Company A's data will be afforded 100% redundancy to an alternate site within 2 hours upon outage.* *Upon an unscheduled outage, disaster, or "Act of God"[19], all (100%) Level 1 data in Company A's Business Continuity Plan (BCP) will be accessible within 6 hours. 70% of the Level 2 data will be accessible within 12 hours. (Less costly option example).*
1	X	Service Reliability	*The CSP is expected to provide all services within in the CSLA at an overall rate of 98.5%?*

Sample Checklist Entries

The second column, **Y?,** is offered as a binary decision for organizational leadership whether it should or should not be included in the CSLA; legal should always be consulted about explicit jurisdictional terminology or language specific to any final version of the CSLA. The remaining columns are self-explanatory. The suggested metric is offered to provide initial language for the CSLA.

There are several controls that cannot be universally suggested. As described, it will require further analysis, for example, **"how many users can access the public-facing webserver without crashing it?"** Further data analysis will be required to include historical data from the organization and potential statistical models that can extrapolate requirements more precisely; these should only be considered notional suggestions.

Security Service Level Objectives (SSLO)

Service Reliability

PRI	Y?	SLO	Suggested Metric
		Level of Redundancy	*Upon a scheduled or unscheduled outage, Company A's data will be afforded 100% redundancy to an alternate site within 2 hours upon outage.* *Upon an unscheduled outage, disaster, or "Act of God", all (100%) Level 1 data in Company A's Business Continuity Plan (BCP) will be accessible within 6 hours. 70% of the Level 2 data will be accessible within 12 hours. (Less costly option example).*
		Service Reliability	*The CSP is expected to provide all services within in the CSLA at an overall rate of 98.5%?* *The CSP is expected to provide all services within in the CSLA at an overall rate of 95%? (Less costly)*

Authentication & Authorization (A&A)

PRI	Y?	SLO	Suggested Metric
		User Authentication and Identity Assurance Level	*The CSP will ensure a 100% Level of Assurance (LOA) for the access to Company A's data and services housed within the CSP.* [The LOA may be based on relevant standards like NIST SP 800-63 (Electronic Authentication Guidelines), ISO/IEC 29115 (Entity Authentication Assurance Framework) or the Kantara Initiative's Identity Assurance Framework (IAF).]

		Authentication	*The CSP will support a Two-factor authentication (2FA) process using hard tokens (cards or security fobs) approved by Company A prior to service activation.* *The CSP will support a Two-factor authentication (2FA) process use Secure Message Service (SMS) to support a non-hard token solution using company smart phones. Company A must approve this capability prior to service activation.*
		Mean Time Required to Revoke User Access	*The CSP will revoke user access to cloud services within 6 hours using a Remedy trouble ticket and confirm all revocations weekly in a report to Company A's Chief Information Security Officer (CISO).*
		User Access Storage Protection	*The CSP will ensure all user access credentials are protected by FIPS 140-2 approved encryption.*
		Third Party Authentication Support	*Company A's third-party subcontractors and consultants will be afforded the same authentication mechanisms as regular employees.*

Cryptography (Encryption)

PRI	Y?	SLO	Suggested Metric
		Cryptographic Brute Force Resistance	*The CSP will provide FIPS 140-2 encryption for all company data; it will ensure that the **Advanced Encryption Standard** (AES) is used with a key length of at least 256 kilobyte (kb).* *The CSP will provide the infrastructure and support to use "Blockchain" as a solution and must also be approved by FIPS 140-2.*

		Key Access Control Policy	*The CSP will provide FIPS 140-2 encryption of a minimum key length 256 kb for all cryptographic keys used for cloud service access, data, capabilities and assets.*
		Cryptographic Hardware Module Protection Level	*The CSP will provide a hardware-based module solution that is FIPS 140-2 approved to support all cloud service access, data, and capabilities.*

Security Incident Management and Reporting

PRI	Y?	SLO	Suggested Metric
		Percentage of Timely Incident Reports	*The CSP will report all the following incidents within 72 hours and meet a 90% on time report rate based upon this standard. The CSP will classify the following as major incidents but is not limited to these categories alone. Reporting will occur upon recognition by the CSP's Security Operation Center (SOC) personnel and Company A's SOC will log all reported incidents for record:* • *Distributed/Denial of Service (D/DOS) attacks* • *Unauthorized intrusions which may include the destruction, modification or exfiltration of any Company A data.* • *Insider Threats where the individual or individuals have or have not accessed Company A's data.* *ALSO, all incidents will be reported to the Department of Homeland Security's (DHS) Computer Emergency Response Team (CERT) (https://www.us-cert.gov/forms/report) within 5-business days and meet this standard at a rate of 100%.*
		Percentage of Timely Incident Resolutions	*The CSP will resolve security incidents within 96 hours and meet a 98.5% on-time resolution rate that includes all actions to reduce or eliminate the threat. This may include updates security patched, configuration updates per applicable STIG update, or additional mitigation factors such as physical security controls or other technical solution.*

Logging and Monitoring

PRI	Y?	SLO	Suggested Metric
		Logging Parameters	*The CSP will record, maintain, archive and make available all logs quarterly to the Company A CISO:* • *Operating System (OS) Logs* • *Database Logs* • *System Logs* • *Backup Logs (can add others as necessary or needed)*
		Log Access Availability	*The CSP will provide full access to all logs (as designated above) either quarterly as agreed or on an ad hoc basis within 72 hours upon request.* [This could be used to provide CSLA contract oversight quality control or support suspected activities that may impact company data adversely.]
		Logs Retention Period	*The logs (as designated above) are subject to National Archive and Records Administration (NARA) retention rules and will be retained for a period of X by the CSP.* *The logs (as designated above) will be retained for at least 5 years.*

Security Auditing

PRI	Y?	SLO	Suggested Metrics
		Certifications Applicable	*The CSP will provide and maintain its FEDRAMP certification (at minimum) and provide it to Company A's Legal Office 30-days prior to cloud service activation. It will include the expiration date and renewal period.* *The CSP will provide an independently assessed certification of its operations and facilities from the following audit companies: Audit 1, Audit 2, or Audit 3, nationally recognized NIST SP 800-XXX auditors, for the purposes of cloud service*

			operations with expiration date and renewal period.

Vulnerability Management

PRI	Y?	SLO	Suggested Metric
		Percentage of Timely Vulnerability Corrections	*The CSP will provide a report monthly to Company A's CISO the total number of vulnerabilities corrected. These will include all recurring application, OS, and security patches. It will also include all related STIG updates that the CSP corrects based on Security Resource Guides (SRG) and STIG updates. This will include the overall percentage completed versus the percentage not completed during the reporting period.* [Monthly may be designated as the first or last business day of the month. Weekly may be required on an ad hoc basis when a new vulnerability (zero-day[22]) that occurs that requires greater review by both the CSC and CSP].
		Percentage of Timely Vulnerability Reports	*The CSP will provide completed "vulnerability" reports No Later Than (NLT) the last business day of the month. Receipt will be based upon email timestamp and delivery to Company A's SOC. The CSP will provide the percentage of on time reports for the previous month.*
		Reports of Vulnerability Corrections	*The CSP will provide a report the last business of the month the total number of vulnerability corrections and include the mechanism (e.g., patch, policy, etc.) that corrects the vulnerability to a state of "corrected."* *The CSP will provide a POAM for all vulnerabilities unmet with a course of action, any milestones, and expected date of completion or correction.* *[There should be no partial correction of a vulnerability; there is no "partial credit." A Plan of Action and*

---

[22] These are attacks where there is no current security patch and sometimes requires other actions by government supported organizations and corporations. These will often require some level of near-immediate action; the government may direct everyone, including NIST 800-171 authorized businesses, report their status to the Contract Officer by an established deadline.

			Milestones (POAM) will be submitted with the report for any unmet security controls.]

Governance

PRI	Y?	SLO	SLO Description
		Baseline Configuration Control	*The CSP will provide baseline update documents quarterly or semi-annually to capture all configuration changes for the previous period. This should include an updated System Security Plan (SSP) or equivalent document that includes at a minimum hardware and software lists and physical network topologies.* [This should be an ongoing effort where the CSP advises of their configuration changes that may impact the CSC's operations, or may include extended services by the CSP to maintain documentation management on behalf of the CSC.]
		Maintain an Audit Change Information System	*The CSP will provide quarterly a report of all change requests received and implemented during the previous reporting period. This includes recurring (e.g., patching) security changes. Non-implemented changes need not be reported.*
		Percentage of Timely Cloud Service Change Notifications	*The CSP will conduct and document a Security Impact Assessment (SIA) for all non-standard changes (e.g., security and application update patches). This should address whether the changes are: 1) "security relevant," and 2) do not adversely impact the CSC by impacting its operational state.*

Service Changes

PRI	Y?	SLO	Suggested Metric
		Cloud Service Change	*The CSP will provide all no-cost service changes within 72 hours upon approval by CSP's leadership (Chief Operating Officer, President, etc.)* *Service changes that increase costs to Company A must be reported to Company A's Legal Department and afforded 30-days to review and discuss cost changes that may or may not be in accordance with current contract or CSLA in effect.*
		Reporting Notifications	*The CSP will report all planned service changes within 30 days.*
		Percentage of Timely Cloud Service Change Notifications	*The CSP will provide monthly (or, quarterly) the total number of service changes and the percentage meeting the 30-day reporting period requirement.*

Performance Service Level Objectives

Availability

PRI	Y?	SLO	Suggested Metric
		Level of Uptime (Often termed "availability")	*The CSP will report monthly the percentage of "uptime" over the total possible available time.* [Uptime excludes scheduled maintenance periods.]
		Percentage of Successful Requests	*The CSP will monitor and track the total number of requests to Company A's "Widget" database and "Global" public-facing website with the percentage of identified (log files) reporting successful completion and the percentage of errors based upon data calls not being met for these critical cloud services.*
		Percentage of Timely Service Provisioning Requests	*The CSP will report the percentage of satisfactorily provisioned CSP services. These will include, for example:* • *Storage* • *Account Access* • *Elevated (privileged) account access* • *Enhanced processing* • *Cybersecurity Sandbox area* • *Honeypots*

Response Time

PRI	Y?	SLO	Suggested Metric
		Average Response Time	*The CSP will meet the following response times based upon designated urgency states for Company A:* • *Tier 1: 24-hour response (basic services)* • *Tier 2: 12-hour response (elevated; potential security event, corporate officer assistance, etc.)* • *Tier 3: 2-hour response (emergency; designated security incident or catastrophic functionality loss related to or suspected with CSP services)*

		Maximum Response Time	*The maximum response times for the CSP are:*
			• *Tier 1: 48 hours*
			• *Tier 2: 24 hours*
			• *Tier 3: 3.5 hours*

Capacity

PRI	Y?	SLO	Suggested Metric
		Number of Simultaneous Connections	*The CSP will allow for x number of simultaneous connections to Company A's major services and y number for basic services.* **[Determining the number of current connections can be analyzed by the company, agency, or CSP based upon past data and industry standards; these numbers will require greater analytic efforts on the part of the company or agency before entering (or requiring this service) as part of a CSLA].**
		Number of Simultaneous Cloud Service Users	*The CSP will allow for x number of simultaneous cloud service users to Company A's major services and y number for basic services.* [Historic and industry specific data analysis required]
		Maximum Resource Capacity	*The CSP will afford a required data storage amount of 15 TB and processing memory of z CPU cores daily.* [Historic and industry specific data analysis required]
		Service Throughput	*The CSP will process the following requests in the specified period of requests per minute:* • *Financial applications: Minimum 500; maximum 1500.* • *Human Resource applications: Minimum 50; maximum 200.* • *Public Website: Minimum 50,000* • *Company A Intranet: Minimum 2500* [Historic and industry specific data analysis required]

Capability Indicators

PRI	Y?	SLO	Suggested Metric
		External Connectivity	*The CSP will provide access to:* • *Company B's Ordering System with CSP #2 at 98% availability rate* • *Company C's Travel System, an Extranet Site (outside of its corporate firewall), at 95% availability.*

Support

PRI	Y?	SLO	Suggested Metric
		Support Hours	*The CSP will provide a 24x7 Help Desk to include a special desk for corporate officers and senior managers*
		Support Responsiveness	*The CSP will adhere to the following maximum time to acknowledge a customer inquiry or request of 24 hours. This will include opening a trouble-ticket and providing electronic feedback to the individual at the same time.* [It is typical for responsiveness to vary depending on the complexity and severity level of the issue]
		Resolution Time	*The CSP will resolve customer requests based upon the following Tiered designations and assuming the resolution is directly related to the approved CSLA:* • *Tier 1 [basic]: 48 hours* • *Tier 2 [intermediate]: 48-72 hours* • *Tier 3 [advanced/Original Equipment Manufacturer (OEM)-level]: 72-96 hours*

Reversibility and the Termination Process

PRI	Y?	SLO	Suggested Metric
		Data Retrieval Period	*The CSP must be able to provide data retrieval of all files, databases, and archive records that that DOES NOT include audit records for a minimum of 2 years to meet current federal data retention standards.* *The CSP will provide data retrieval of all audit logs[23] specific to system logs for a period of a minimum of 2 years.*
		Data Retention Period	*The CSP may retain all Company A backup copies for a period of two years to aid in any future legal or law enforcement requests made by the COO or CISO in writing.* *The CSP is required to surrender currently stored backup copies within 60 days of termination. Furthermore, all remaining data, files, archival copies, etc., stored within the agreed to cloud hosting environment within 60 days, and provide a certification by senior CSP management that the action has been fully accomplished.* [Furthermore, the company or agency is obliged to consult with legal what the statutory requirements are for the jurisdiction. US companies may check www.nara.gov for required retention standards.]
		Residual Data Retention	*The CSP will delete and certify 100% deletion of any "derived data" within 60 days. Notification will be provided to Company A's COO or CISO.*

---

[23] An audit log and associated files should be requested to determine whether there has been any unauthorized access during the termination period. While not typical, it most likely will incur additional costs.

Data Management Service Level Objectives

Data Classification

PRI	Y?	SLO	Suggested Metrics
		Cloud Service Customer Data use by the Provider	*The CSP is barred from using any CSC data without the express permission of the customer. Derived data (externals) should be limited and not violate any current international, US law or regulation.* *The CSP is specifically authorized to the Global Address List (GAL) for the express purpose of determining CSC users, their locations, and phone numbers to provide direct help desk support pursuant to normal help desk support in accordance with the CSLA.*
		Cloud Service Derived Data Use	*The CSP will may create derived data for limited workload and trending analysis. This may include, for example:* • *Tier level call* • *Number of minutes on phone with customer* • *Number of hours/days to resolve an issue* • *Number of times an issue needs to be referred for CSP external support (Tier 3) with subcontractors and OEM entities (e.g., Microsoft, Symantec, etc.* • *Age of open tickets* • *CSP support staff specific workload statistics* *The CSC may request all reports derived in support of other measurable events required under the CSLA.* *The CSP will provide bi-annual reports on the current types and kinds of derived currently being collected and retained by the CSP on an ad hoc basis. The CSP is required to provide this information within 30 days of the request.*

Cloud Service Customer Data Mirroring Backup & Restore

PRI	Y?	SLO	Suggested Metric
		Data Mirroring Latency	*The CSP will mirror all data within 12 hours (highly sensitive data) to the primary storage location or 48 hours (basic data) to ensure future restoration as needed or required.* [This time should always be based upon the sensitivity of the data if lost or compromised]
		Data Backup Method	*The CSP will provide the following backup method per the CSLA* • *The "Other Cloud Storage" CSP located offsite and agreed to per the CSLA.* • *Or, backup drives approved by the CISO and having DAR compliant software providing FIPS 140-2 encryption* • *Any exceptions may only be approved by Company A's COO or CISO and must be in writing and signed.*
		Data Backup Frequency	*The CSP will conduct complete all data backups weekly. Incremental backups will occur daily during off peak areas based upon Company A's Headquarters location and time zone.*
		Backup Retention Time	*The CSP will provide backups in cases of data restoration requirements within 5 business days. For the purposes of legal or law enforcement actions, the COO or CISO will provide ad hoc requests in writing for no later than 48 hours.* [This type action may require an additional fee; this cost should be identified as part of the contract and CSLA process].
		Backup Generations	*The CSP will maintain "First in, first out" (FIFO) scheme of at least 3 generations of backups: 1) previous version 1 [oldest], 2) previous version 2 [next oldest], and 3) current version [next to move to offline storage]. This will avoid the introduction Refers to the number of backup generations available for use in data restoration.* [A "First in, first out" (FIFO) scheme suffers from the possibility of data loss. If an error is introduced into the data, but the problem is not identified until several generations later than

			the error will be undetected. "It would then be useful to have at least one [in this case 2] older versions of the data as it would not [likely] have the error."[24]
		Maximum Data Restoration time	*The CSP's maximum restoration time will be no greater than 8 business days.*
		Percentage of Successful Data Restorations	*The CSP will provide success rates (%) for all data restoration activities over the past month. This will also include the number of data restorations performed without errors (Six Sigma or greater—See Chart Below) over the total number of data restorations.*

DPMO = Defects per Million Opportunities

- A more sensitive indicator than % yield or % good

Sigma	Defects	Yield	DPMO
1	69.1%	30.9%	691,462
2	30.8%	69.1%	308,538
3	6.7%	93.3%	66,807
4	0.62%	99.38%	6,210
5	0.02%	99.977%	233
6	0.0003%	99.9997%	3.4

Standard Sigma Defects/Errors Chart

---

[24] https://en.wikipedia.org/wiki/Backup_rotation_scheme

Data Lifecycle

PRI	Y?	SLO	Suggested Metric
		Data Deletion Type	*The CSP will use moderate sanitization methods as defined by NIST 800-88 and approved by Company A's CISO.* [Deletion may include 'weak' to 'strong' sanitization methods[25] as suggested by NIST based up data sensitivity.]
		Percentage of Timely Effective Deletions	*The CSP will provide a monthly report of number (#) and percent (%) successful deletions over the total number of deletion requests.*
		Percentage of Tested Storage Retrievability	*The CSP will verify percent of deletions and will verify 20% of the data deleted. Further, the CSP will report the percent of the 20% tested where the data was retrievable (failed) and report that number and percentage to Company A monthly.*

Data Portability

PRI	Y?	SLO	Suggested Metric
		Data Portability Format	*The CSC will use the following electronic formats: (those designated by the CSP that can be transferred to/accessed from the cloud service.)* [This will be typically discussed pre-CSLA acceptance. The CSP must be able to import and manipulate these inbound files within its operating systems and application environment to meet CSC requirements and functionalities.]
		Data Portability Interface	*The CSP will define the required mechanisms (A, B, C, etc.) that will be used to transfer cloud service customer data to and from the cloud service.*

---

[25]Refer to "NIST Special Publication 800-88: Guidelines for Media Sanitization".

			[This specification potentially includes the transport protocols, APIs or other mechanism that is supported, and provided by the CSP prior to CSLA acceptance]
		Data Transfer Rate	*The CSP will provide a minimum data rate of 100 GB per second (for example only) for cloud service customer data that can be transferred to/from the cloud service using the mechanism(s) stated in the data interface.* **[This will require the review of historical data transfer usage and analysis of industry specific requirements for data transfer rates within/to a cloud environment].**

Personal Data Protection Service Level Objectives

Codes of Conduct, Standards and Certification

PRI	Y?	SLO	Suggested Metric
		Applicable Data Protection Codes of Conduct, Standards, Certifications	*The CSP will ensure all employees actively supporting Company A's cloud instantiation and operations have executed a "code of conduct" statement as defined by industry standards. Notification of 100% compliance is required within 60 days of CLSA ratification.* [This may be required for both the CSP and CSC subject to jurisdictional requirements, restrictions, and cybersecurity framework adopted, e.g., NIST 800-53, NIST 800-171, etc.]

Purpose Specification

PRI	Y?	SLO	Suggested Metric
		Processing Purposes	*The CSP will provide all processing purposes (if any) which are beyond those requested by the customer acting as a controller prior to CSLA ratification.*

Data Minimization

PRI	Y?	SLO	Suggested Metric
		Temporary Data Retention Period	*The CSP will report within a maximum of 60-days that retained temporary data, after identification that the data is no longer usable/required will be deleted and the completion will be reported to Company A CISO.*
		Cloud Service Customer Data Retention Period	*The CSP will report within a maximum of 60 days regarding cloud customer data destruction by the CSP after Company A's request to delete the data or based upon termination of the contract/CSLA.*

Use, Retention and Disclosure Limitations

PRI	Y?	SLO	Suggested Metric
		Number of Customer Data Law Enforcement Disclosures	*The CSP will provide quarterly updates regarding the number of Company A's personal **data disclosures** processed and provided to law enforcement subject to legal authority where such disclosures are permitted by law.* *The CSP will provide ad hoc reporting regarding the number of Company A's personal data disclosures to law enforcement subject to legal authority to include all warrants where such disclosures are permitted by law and will have 48 hours to provide to Company A's Legal Department.*
		Number of Personal Data Disclosure Notifications	*The CSP will provide quarterly updates regarding the number of Company A's personal data **notifications received** from law enforcement authorities subject to legal authority to include all warrants where such disclosures are permitted by law.*

Transparency and Notice

PRI	Y?	SLO	Suggested Metric
		List of Tier 1 Subcontractors	*The CSP will provide a list of all of its Tier 1 subcontractors upon CSLA execution and provide quarterly updates regarding the addition or deletion of subcontractors directly or indirectly involved with the care, maintenance, and provisioning of Company A's cloud environment.*
		Special Categories of Data	*The CSP will provide a listing 30-days prior to execution of the CSLA of specific categories of personal data (if any), e.g. health-related or financial data or otherwise sensitive data, that the cloud service is suitable for processing, according to applicable standards or regulations. (If not provided, it may*

PRI	Y?	SLO	Suggested Metric
			be grounds for unilateral termination of CSLA and its associated contract.

Accountability

PRI	Y?	SLO	Suggested Metric
		Personal Data Breach Policy	*The CSP will provide its "personal data breach" policy upon CSLA execution and will provide updates annually.*

		Documentation	*The CSP will provide the following standard cybersecurity documents based upon NIST 800-XXX requirements (for example:*
			• *System Security Plan (SSP)*
			• *All Plans of Action and Milestones (POAM)*
			• *Privacy Impact Assessments (PIA)*
			• *Security Assessment (Test) Plan (SAP)*
			• *Internal or externally provided Security Assessment Reports (SAR)*
			• *FEDRAMP certifications*
			• *Standard Operating Procedures(SOP) (to include, but not limited to):*
			   ○ *Access requests*
			   ○ *Designation of data protection officers*
			   ○ *Required cybersecurity certifications requirements*

Geographical Location of Cloud Service Customer Data

PRI	Y?	SLO	Suggested Metric
		Data Geolocation List	*The CSP will provide the specified location or locations (specific geographically) where the cloud service customer data may be stored and processed 60-days prior to CSLA execution.*

		Data Geolocation Selection	The CSP will advise the CSC within 5 business days of any changes in available new CSP geographical locations (jurisdictions) that the CSC has either a no-cost or cost option to shift data and other capacity to these new sites.

Intervenability

PRI	Y?	SLO	Suggested Metric
		Access Request Response Time	The CSP shall notify the CSC immediately, and allow for a 14-day review of provided information necessary to allow the CSC to respond to access requests by the data subjects. The CSC has 14 business days to approve or disapprove the access; this stipulation requires the CSP to support the exercise of Company A data subject rights in a timely and efficient manner.

APPENDIX A -- Terminology

Term	Definition
Application Programming Interface (API)	The collection of invocation methods and associated parameters used by a certain (part of) cloud service or software component to request actions from and otherwise interact with another cloud service or software component.
Auditability	The capability of supporting a systematic, independent and documented process for obtaining audit evidence and evaluating it objectively to determine the extent to which audit criteria are fulfilled.
Availability	The property of being accessible and usable upon demand by an authorized entity.
Cloud Computing	A paradigm for enabling network access to a scalable and elastic pool of shareable physical or virtual resources with self-service provisioning and administration on-demand.[11] Examples of resources include servers, operating systems, networks, software, applications, and storage equipment.
Cloud Infrastructure	The collection of hardware, software and other related goods and resources that enables the provision of cloud services.
Cloud Service	One or more capabilities offered via cloud computing invoked using a defined interface.
Cloud Service Customer	A party which is in a business relationship for using cloud services, for this document not being consumers. NOTE – A business relationship may not necessarily imply financial agreements or similar arrangements.
Cloud Service Customer Data	class of data objects under the control, by legal or other reasons, of the cloud service customer that were input to the cloud service, or resulted from exercising the capabilities of the cloud service by or on behalf of the cloud service customer via the published interface of the cloud service

Cloud Service Derived Data	Class of data objects under cloud service provider control that are derived because of interaction with the cloud service by the cloud service customer

Cloud service derived data includes log data containing records of who used the service, at what times, which functions, types of data involved and so on. It can also include information about the numbers of authorized users and their identities. It can also include any configuration or customization data, where the cloud service has such configuration and customization capabilities. |
| *Cloud Service Level Objective (SLO)* | Target for a given attribute of a cloud service that can be expressed quantitatively or qualitatively. |
| *Cloud Service Provider (CSP)* | A party which makes cloud services available. |
| *Cloud Service Provider Data* | class of data objects, specific to the operation of the cloud service, under the control of the cloud service provider

Cloud service provider data includes but is not limited to resource configuration and utilization information, cloud service specific virtual machine, storage and network resource allocations, overall data center configuration and utilization, physical and virtual resource failure rates, operational costs and so on. |
| *Cloud Service User* | natural person, or entity acting on their behalf, associated with a cloud service customer that uses cloud services

Examples of such entities include devices and applications. |
Cloud SLA Life Cycle	Service level agreements life cycle i.e.; assessment, negotiation, contracting, operation, amendment, escalation and termination, and other arrangements and matters.
Cloud SLA (CSLA)	Documented agreement between the cloud service provider and cloud service customer that identifies services and cloud service level objectives (SLOs).
Cryptographic Key Management	Key management is the management of cryptographic keys in a cryptosystem. This includes dealing with the generation, exchange, storage, use, and replacement of keys, as well as cryptographic protocol. It includes cryptographic protocol design, key servers, user procedures, and other relevant protocols.

Data	Data of any form, nature or structure, that can be created, uploaded, inserted in, collected or derived from or with cloud services and/or cloud computing, including without limitation proprietary and non-proprietary data, confidential and non-confidential data, non-personal and personal data, as well as other human readable or machine-readable data.

Data Controller	The natural or legal person, public authority, agency or any other body which alone or jointly with others determines the purposes and means of the processing of personal data.
Data Format	One or more formats in which the data is in one or more phases of its data lifecycle.
Data Integrity	The property of protecting the accuracy and completeness of assets.
Data Intervenability	The capability of a cloud service provider to support the cloud service customer in facilitating exercise of data subjects' rights. Note: Data subjects' rights include without limitation access, rectification, erasure of the data subjects' personal data. They also include the objection to processing of the personal data when it is not carried out in compliance with the applicable legal requirements.
Data Life Cycle	The handling of data that commonly includes six (6) phases, (1) create/derive, (2) store, (3) use/process, (4) share, (5) archive, (6) destroy.[26]
Data Location	The geographic location(s) where personal data may be stored or otherwise processed by the cloud service provider.
Data Portability	Ability to easily transfer data from one system to another without being required to re-enter data.
Data Processor	A natural or legal person, public authority, agency or any other body which processes Personal data on behalf of the Data controller.
Data Protection	The employment of technical, organizational and legal measures to achieve the goals of data security (confidentiality, integrity and availability), transparency, intervenability and portability, as well as compliance with the relevant legal framework.

---

[26] https://cloudsecurityalliance.org/download/security-guidance-for-critical-areas-of-focus-in-cloud-computing-v3/

Data Subject	An identified or identifiable natural person, being an identifiable person is one who can be identified, directly or indirectly, by reference to an identification number or to one or more factors specific to his physical, physiological, mental, economic, cultural or social identity.
Hybrid Cloud	Deployment model of cloud computing using at least two different cloud deployment models.
Identity Assurance	The ability of a relying party to determine, with some level of certainty, that a claim to a identity made by some entity can be trusted to actually be the claimant's true, accurate and correct identity.
Incident Notification and Transparency	Notifications and transparency about incidents under the SLA that may be required as per (a) mandatory law and legislation (such as under the EU Network and Information Security ('NIS') Directive), and/or (b) contractual arrangement.

Information Security	The preservation of confidentiality, integrity and availability of information.
Infrastructure as a Service (IaaS)	The capability provided to the cloud service customer is to provision processing, storage, networks, and other fundamental computing resources where the cloud service customer can deploy and run arbitrary software, which can include operating systems and applications. The cloud service customer does not manage or control the underlying cloud infrastructure but has control over operating systems, storage, and deployed applications; and possibly limited control of select networking components (e.g., host firewalls).
Incident Management	The processes for detecting, reporting, assessing, responding to, dealing with, and learning from information security incidents.
Metric	A metric is a defined measurement method and measurement scale, which is used in relation to a quantitative service level objective.
Personal Data	Any information relating to an identified or identifiable natural person ('data subject'); an identifiable person is one who can be identified, directly or indirectly, by reference to an identification number or to one or more factors specific to his physical, physiological, mental, economic, cultural or social identity.

Platform as a Service (PaaS)	The capability provided to the cloud service customer is to deploy onto the cloud infrastructure customer-created or acquired applications created using programming languages, libraries, services, and tools supported by the CSP. The cloud service customer does not manage or control the underlying cloud infrastructure including network, servers, operating systems, or storage, but has control over the deployed.
Private Cloud	The cloud infrastructure is provisioned for exclusive use by a single organization comprising multiple cloud service customers (e.g., business units). It may be owned, managed, and operated by the organization, a third party, or some combination of them, and it may exist on or off premises.
Processing of Personal Data	Any operation or set of operations which is performed upon Personal data, whether by automatic means, such as collection, recording, organization, storage, adaptation or alteration, retrieval, consultation, use, disclosure by transmission, dissemination or otherwise making available, alignment or combination, blocking, erasure or destruction.
Public Cloud	The cloud infrastructure is provisioned for open use by the public. It may be owned, managed, and operated by a business, academic, or government organization, or some combination of them. It exists on the premises of the CSP and/or its suppliers.
Response Time	Time interval between a cloud service customer-initiated event (stimulus) and a cloud service provider-initiated event in response to that stimulus.
Representational State Transfer (*REST*)	Representational state transfer (REST) is a software architectural style consisting of a coordinated set of architectural constraints applied to components, connectors, and data elements, within a distributed hypermedia system.
Reversibility	Process for cloud service customers to retrieve their cloud service customer data and application artefacts and for the cloud service provider to delete all cloud service customer data as well as contractually specified cloud service derived data after an agreed period.
Sensitive Data	Any classified, personal, proprietary or confidential information or data of any form, nature or structure, that can be created, uploaded, inserted in, collected or derived from or with cloud services and/or cloud computing whose access, use, disclosure or processing is subject to restriction either by applicable law or contact.[27]

---

[27] This includes (but is not limited to) sensitive data pursuant to the 95/46/EC directive for the protection of personal data, for which the definition of the directive applies.

Software as a Service (SaaS)	The capability provided to the cloud service customer is to use the cloud service provider's applications running on a cloud infrastructure. The applications are accessible from various client devices through either a thin client interface, such as a web browser (e.g. web-based email), or a program interface. The cloud service customer does not manage or control the underlying cloud infrastructure including network, servers, operating systems, storage, or even individual application capabilities, except for limited user-specific application configuration settings.
Temporary Data	Data or a data set that is created during the operation of the cloud service and becomes unused after a predefined period.
Vulnerability	A weakness of an asset or group of assets, e.g. software or hardware related, that can be exploited by one or more threats.
XaaS	A collective term of diverse but re-useable components, including without limitation infrastructure, platforms, data, software, middleware, hardware or other goods, made available as a service with use of cloud computing.

APPENDIX B--Sample Cloud Service Level Agreement (CSLA) with Suggested Comments/Actions

1. Purpose and Scope

The Objective of this "Service Level Agreement" (hereinafter "SLA" for short) is to define the reference parameters for the provision of the [CLOUD SERVICE PROVIDER] service (hereinafter "Service" for short) and for monitoring the level of quality provided. The objective of the SLA is also to define the rules of interaction between [CSP] and the Customer. This SLA is an integral part of the Contract completed between [CSP] and the Customer with the rules defined in [OTHER GENERALIZED PROVISIONING DOCUMENTS, IF REQUIRED]. This SLA applies separately to each Customer and for each Contract.

2. Validity and Duration – Modifications and Replacements

This SLA shall enter into force for an indefinite period for each Customer after the conclusion of each Contract and shall end with the termination of the Contract to which it relates. [CSP] reserves the right to change or replace it several times [NOTE: CUSTOMER HAS AN OPPORTUNITY TO LIMIT CHANGES AND SHOULD ALSO REQUIRE AT LEAST A TWO_WEEK NOTICE OF PENDING CHANGES] during the Contract and at any time. Changes made to the SLA or the new SLA - replacement of the previous one - shall always enter into force for an indefinite [SHOULD ALWAYS BE NEGOTIABLE; LIMIT IT TO THE FULL TERM OF THE CONTRACT OR AT SPECIFICED OPTION PERIODS OF THE CONTRACT] period or until the next change or replacement, from the date of their publication on the page [CAN INCLUDE REFERENCE DOCUMENT OR PUBLIC CSP WEB PAGE FOR CHANGES IN THE TERM OF SERVICES]; However, in this case the Customer shall be given the opportunity to withdraw from the contract according to the rules defined in the contract [THIS SHOULD BE A SEPARATE DOCUMENT] within thirty days of the date of publication of the change and/or the replacement of the SLA. In the event of a withdrawal by the Customer the rules laid down in the Conditions of Service Provision applies.

3.   Operational Functionality

3.1. [CSP] will make every reasonable effort [REMEMBER: IF STANDARDS ARE NOT MET, THERE SHOULD BDE A FINANCIAL IMPACT TO THE CSP DEFINED IN THE MAIN CONTRACT] to ensure maximum availability of the virtual infrastructure created and allocated by the Customer and, at the same time, the observance of the following operational functionality parameters:

A) Resources of the Data Center via which the Service is provided:

- Ninety-none percent (%) uptime on an annual basis for electricity and/or air conditioning;
- The switching off the virtual infrastructure created and allocated by the Customer caused by a general lack of the power supply and/or air conditioning is a malfunction for which, based on its duration, by way of compensation the Customer will be due credit [ENSURE THIS AREA IS REVIEWED BY LEGAL REPRESENTATIVES] determined in accordance with [CONTRACT, OR OTHER SUPPORT DOCUMENT] of this SLA;
- 99.95% uptime on an annual basis and accessibility via the Internet to the virtual infrastructure created and allocated by the Customer;
- The complete inaccessibility via the Internet to the virtual infrastructure created and allocated by the Customer for a total time longer than that determined by the Uptime guaranteed parameter by [CSP] is a malfunction for which, based on its duration, by way of compensation the Customer will be due credit according to [DEFINED DOCUMENT] of this SLA.

B) Virtual infrastructure created and allocated by the Customer:
- 99.95% uptime on an annual basis, for the availability of physical nodes (servers) hosting the virtual infrastructure;
- The failure of the virtual infrastructure created and allocated by the Customer - for a total time longer than that determined by the Uptime guaranteed parameter by [CSP] - caused by failures and/or anomalies of the physical nodes is a malfunction for which, based on its duration, by way of compensation the Customer will be due credit according to [DEFINED DOCUMENT] of this SLA.

3.2. If the Customer purchases the [EXTENDED SUPPORT] via [CONTRACT/SLA MECHANISM], [CSP] will make every reasonable effort to ensure maximum availability of the virtual infrastructure created and allocated by the Customer and, at the same time, the observance of the following operational function parameters:

A) Resources of the Data Center through which the Service is provided:
- 100% uptime on an annual basis for power supply and/or air conditioning;
- The switching off the virtual infrastructure created and allocated by the Customer caused by a general lack of power supply and/or air conditioning is a malfunction which, based on its duration, entitles the Customer, by way of compensation, to the credit established in accordance with [DEFINED DOCUMENT] of this SLA;
- 99.8% uptime on an annual basis, of accessibility via the internet to the virtual infrastructure created and allocated by the Customer;
- The complete inaccessibility via the Internet to the virtual infrastructure created and allocated by the Customer for a total amount of time longer than the amount of time determined by the Uptime parameter guaranteed by [CSP] is a malfunction which,

based on its duration, entitles the Customer, by way of compensation, to the credit established in accordance with [DEFINED DOCUMENT] of this SLA.

B) Virtual infrastructure created and allocated by the Customer:
  - 99.8% uptime on an annual basis, for the availability of physical nodes (servers) hosting the virtual infrastructure;
  - Failure of the virtual infrastructure created and allocated by the Customer - for a total amount of time longer than the amount of time determined by the Uptime parameter guaranteed by [CSP] - caused by failures and/or anomalies of the physical nodes is a malfunction which, based on its duration, entitles the Customer, by way of compensation, to the credit established in accordance with [DEFINED DOCUMENT] of this SLA.

4.   Planned Maintenance

4.1. Time for planned maintenance is not counted in the Uptime calculation. Planned maintenance concerns activities regularly carried out by [CSP] to maintain the functionality of the Data Center resources by means of which the Service and the physical nodes that host the virtual infrastructure is provided; both ordinary and extraordinary.

4.2. The implementation of the maintenance [GENERAL MAINTENANCE ONLY; THIS SHOULD BE DEFINED BY CSP] operations will be communicated to the Customer by [CSP] with at least 48 hours' notice by email sent to the email address indicated in the order phase. [CSP] is committed to making every reasonable effort to carry out the planned maintenance tasks at times with minimal impact to the Customer's virtual infrastructure.

5.   Detecting Failures and Faults

5.1. Any failures and/or faults of the resources of the Data Center by means of which the Service or the physical nodes that host the virtual infrastructure created and allocated by the Customer is provided, shall be reported by the Customer by opening a ticket on the service page [DEFINED LOCATION OR MECHANISM REQUIRED]; for the purposes of awarding credits, however, only malfunctions also confirmed by [CSP; THERE NEEDS TO BE A DISPUTE MECHANISM SUCH AS ARBITRATION THAT IS DEFINED IN THE MAIN CONTRACT BY LEGAL PROFESSIONALS] monitoring system will be taken into consideration.

5.2. Failures or faults can be reported by the Customer to the [CSP] support service 24 hours a day. Any reports received will be promptly forwarded to the technical support strictly respecting the chronological order of receipt.

5.3. Monitoring by [CSP] is carried out using specific software packages that detect and indicate any failures or faults by notifying the support service which operates 24/7, 365 days a year in real-time.

6.   Refunds and Credits

6.1. For the purposes of this SLA [CSP] awards the customer, by way of compensation, with credit equal to 5% [NOTE: REFER THIS TO LEGAL FOR REVIEW] of the total expenditure generated - in thirty days prior to the malfunction or rather in the month previous to the month affected by the malfunction if the Customer has purchased a Service with a monthly plan (such as, by way of example only, [EXTENDED CLOUD SERVICES]) - by the virtual infrastructure concerned by it for each complete portion of fifteen minutes of malfunction beyond the limits set by this SLA, up to a maximum of three (300) hundred minutes[SUGGEST LEGAL REVIEW BASED UPON THE SERVICE TYPE SUPPORTED].

6.2. To be awarded the credit the Customer must contact the [CSP] Support Service by opening a ticket on the website [OR OTHER DEFINED MECHANISM] within 30 days from the end of the Malfunction. Credits awarded by [CSP] will only be issued by crediting the amount to [SPECIFIED COMPANY ACCOUNT OR OTHER DEFINED MEANS TO ACCEPT CREDITS FOR DOWN-TIME ISSUES].

6.3. Notwithstanding the above, it remains in any case understood that during the period of its inactivity, the Service is not generating expense and therefore for this period the corresponding amount provided in the Price List for each of the resources created and allocated by the Customer in the virtual infrastructure will not be deducted from the Top-up; any amount deducted by mistake will be reimbursed by [CSP].

6.4. The Customer agrees and accepts that in case of purchase of a Service with a monthly plan (such as, by way of example only, [EXTENDED SERVICE PLAN], he/she shall not be entitled to any refund from [CSP] for the period of Service inactivity except for the credit referred to in the paragraph 6.1.

7. Applicability Limits

Listed below are the conditions in the presence of which, despite the occurrence of any malfunction, the Customer is not due any compensation provided by the SLA:

- Due to a Force Majeure, i.e. events that, objectively, would prevent [CSP] staff from intervening to perform the tasks set out by the Contract which are [CSP] responsibility (merely by way of example and not exhaustive: strikes and demonstrations which block communication routes; road accidents; wars and acts of terrorism, natural disasters such as flooding, storms, hurricanes, etc.);
- Extraordinary interventions to be carried out urgently at the sole discretion of [CSP] to avoid hazards to safety and/or stability and/or confidentiality and/or integrity of the virtual

infrastructure created and allocated by the Customer and the data and/or information contained therein. Any execution of these measures will be communicated to the Customer via email sent to the email address provided when ordering with less than 48 hours' notice, or at the start of the operations in question or in any case, as soon as possible;

- Unavailability or blocks of the virtual infrastructure created and allocated by the Customer due to:

  1. Incorrect use, incorrect configuration or shut-down commands voluntarily or involuntarily performed by the customer;
  2. Faults and malfunctions of application/management software provided by third parties;
  3. Non-fulfilment or breach of Contract due to the Customer;

- Fault or malfunction of the Service, or their failure or delayed removal or elimination due to non-fulfilment or breach of Contract by the Customer or to an abuse of the Service by the Customer;
- Failure by the virtual infrastructure to connect to the public network voluntarily, or due to the Customer;
- Causes that lead to total or partial inaccessibility of the virtual infrastructure created and allocated by the Customer due to faults in the Internet network beyond [CSP's] perimeter, and therefore beyond its control (merely by way of example, failures or problems).

[SIGNATURE BLOCKS FOR AUTHORIZED REPRESENTATIVE FOR THE CSP TO ACCEPT TERMS OF CSLA]

[SIGNATURE BLOCKS FOR AUTHORIZED REPRESENTATIVE FOR THE CSC TO ACCEPT TERMS OF CSLA]

Selected References

Edwards, J. (2014). DoD's Cloud Security Challenge. *C4ISR Journal*, 29.

Holbrook, E. (2012). Cloud Security. *Risk Management* (59(6)), 12-13.

Intelligence and National Security Alliance (INSA): Cloud Computing Task Force. (2012). *Cloud Computing: Risks, Benefits, and Mission Enhancement for the Intelligence Community [White Paper]*. Retrieved 2014, from http://www.slideshare.net/ kvjacksn/insa-cloud-computing2012final?utm_source=sldeshow02&utm_medium= ssemail&utm_campaign=share_slideshow

International Information Systems Security Certification Consortium (2013). *Official ISC2 ISSAP CBP Training Seminar.* Unknown: International Information Systems Security Certification Consortium.

Konkel, F. (2014). Daring Deal. *Government Executive*, 31-37.

Methodologies Corporation. (2011). Cloud Computing Toolbox Model Language Specifications. Retrieved July 2014, from *Service-Oriented Modeling Framework (tm) (SOMF)*: http://www.modelingconcepts.com/pdf/SOMF_2.1_Cloud_Computing_Toolbox_Model_Langua ge_Specifications.pdf

Nanavati, M., Colp, P., Aiello, B., & Warfield, A. (2014). Cloud Security: A Gathering Storm. *Communications of the ACM*, 70-79. doi:10.1145/2593686

Ogigau-Neamtiu, F. (2012). Cloud Computing Security Issues. Retrieved July 2014, from *Journal of Defense Resources Management*: http://search.proquest.com.nduezproxy.idm.oclc.org/docview/1288095353?accountid=12686

Seffers, G. I. (2013). Committed to Cloud Computing. Retrieved July 2014, from *Signal*: http://search.proquest.com.nduezproxy.idm.oclc.org/docview/1448254779?accountid=12686

Yeluri, R., & Castro-Leon, E. (2014). Building the Infrastructure for Cloud Security: A Solution View. New York, NY: Apress Media, LLC.

About the Author

Mr. Russo is a former Senior Information Security Engineer within the Department of Defense's (DOD) F-35 Joint Strike Fighter program. He has an extensive background in cybersecurity and is an expert in the Risk Management Framework (RMF) and DOD Instruction 8510.01 which implements RMF throughout the DOD and the federal government. He holds both a Certified Information Systems Security Professional (CISSP) certification and a CISSP in information security architecture (ISSAP). He holds a 2017 certification as a Chief Information Security Officer (CISO) from the National Defense University, Washington, DC. He retired from the US Army Reserves in 2012 as the Senior Intelligence Officer.

He is the former CISO at the Department of Education wherein 2016 he led the effort to close over 95% of the outstanding US Congressional and Inspector General cybersecurity shortfall weaknesses spanning as far back as five years.

Mr. Russo is the former Senior Cybersecurity Engineer supporting the Joint Medical Logistics Development Functional Center of the Defense Health Agency (DHA) at Fort Detrick, MD. He led a team of engineering and cybersecurity professionals protecting five major Medical Logistics systems supporting over 200 DOD Medical Treatment Facilities around the globe.

In 2011, Mr. Russo was certified by the Office of Personnel Management as a graduate of the Senior Executive Service (SES) Candidate program.

From 2009 through 2011, Mr. Russo was the Chief Technology Officer at the Small Business Administration (SBA). He led a team of over 100 IT professionals in supporting an intercontinental Enterprise IT infrastructure and security operations spanning 12-time zones; he deployed cutting-edge technologies to enhance SBA's business and information sharing operations supporting the small business community.   Mr. Russo was the first-ever Program Executive Officer (PEO)/Senior Program Manager in the Office of Intelligence & Analysis at Headquarters, Department of Homeland Security (DHS), Washington, DC. Mr. Russo was responsible for the development and deployment of secure Information and Intelligence support systems for OI&A to include software applications and systems to enhance the DHS mission. He was responsible for the program management development lifecycle during his tenure at DHS.

He holds a Master of Science from the National Defense University in Government Information Leadership with a concentration in Cybersecurity and a Bachelor of Arts in Political Science with a minor in Russian Studies from Lehigh University. He holds Level III Defense Acquisition certification in Program Management, Information Technology, and Systems Engineering. He has been a member of the DOD Acquisition Corps since 2001.

Other Books & Articles by the Author

System Security Plan (SSP)
Template & Workbook - NIST-based:
A Supplement to "Blueprint:
Understanding Your
Responsibilities... Mar 13, 2018
by Mark A. Russo CISSP-ISSAP

Hope for a Holy Grail of Continuous Monitoring
THE CYBER EDGE
October 1 2017
By Lt Col. Mark A. Russo, USA (Ret.)

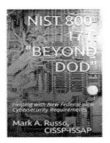

NIST 800-171:Beyond DOD: New
Federal-wide Cybersecurity
Requirements May 5, 2018
by Mark A. Russo CISSP-ISSAP

NIST 800-171: Writing an Effective
Plan of Action & Milestones (POAM):
A Supplement to "Understanding
Your Responsibilities... Apr 6, 2018
by Mark A. Russo CISSP-ISSAP

NOTES: